90 DAY MONEY CHALLENGE

BOOT CAMP
FOR FINANCIAL FITNESS

BRIAN HAMILTON

GORSUCH GRAPHICS, LLC
Baltimore, Maryland

This publication is designed to provide accurate and authoritative information in regard to the subject matter covered. It is sold with the understanding that neither the author nor the publisher is engaged in rendering legal, investment, accounting, or other professional services. If legal advice or other expert assistance is required, the services of a competent professional person should be sought.

Designed by Gorsuch Graphics, LLC.
Manufactured in the United States of America.

For information regarding special discounts for bulk purchases, please visit www.90DayMoneyChallenge.com

ISBN-13: 978-0615469164
ISBN-10:   0615469167

First Edition

To Kerrie, for taking this journey with me

CONTENTS

www.

This symbol appears throughout the book, indicating FREE downloadable materials at www.90DayMoneyChallenge.com

1

SECRETS OF THE RICH

The Victory Lap

It's 7:46AM on Friday and I just parked on South Central Avenue, minutes before I'm due at the office. I rush to put The Club across the steering wheel and quickly grab my brown-bag lunch, sitting beside me in my newly-purchased, 15-year-old beige Honda Accord, which has a lovely corduroy maroon interior.

My co-worker and I refer to this daily one-mile walk to work as our "victory lap." I stopped parking in the $8 per day garage that was right next to the office the day after I sold my much nicer four-year-old Toyota 4-Runner and purchased this little gem.

But none of that matters. Today is the day! It's the day that my wife, Kerrie, and I are making the final payment on my student loan. Today is the day we become completely debt-free! And it feels great! Making a combined income of $100,000 per year, we have eliminated over $52,000 of debt in eight short months. The experience, though intense, was entirely worth it.

More importantly, we changed the way we handled money and had a vision of a much better future. I was the happiest guy in the world!

Boot Camp for Financial Fitness

In the military, boot camp prepares recruits for all elements of service: physical, mental, and emotional. It gives service members the basic tools and confidence necessary to perform the roles that will be asked of them for the duration of their tour. Boot camp is an intense experience. However, about 90% of recruits finish. The purpose of this training isn't to "break" recruits. In fact, the combination of physical training, field exercises, and classroom time makes individuals strong and capable. It's a tough process, but a rewarding one that many service members value for life.

For those who persevere, the journey is life-changing.

Similar to the military, this boot camp is designed to give you the basic tools and confidence necessary to become financially fit. For those who persevere, the journey is life-changing.

Financially Fit

Financially fit is not a number; it's a feeling. What would it *feel like* to be completely out of debt? Do you know what you could do if you had no payments – no car payments, student loan payments, credit card payments, or even house payments? You could retire with dignity. You could leave a legacy and completely change your family tree. You could impact your entire community and maybe even your whole region with the giving you could do. Money gives you the unique ability to completely change your life, the lives of your family, and possibly the world.

Take just a minute right now and think what you would do if money was not an issue. Would you travel across the world? Would you get that car you've always wanted? Would you give like never before?

Money doesn't have to be an issue that stops you from living your dreams. It is really simple to understand how to put yourself in a position where you can really live your dreams, but it is hard to actually do it.

For example, let's look at a couple making $100,000 per year that doesn't have anything in their retirement account right now. If they started investing 15% of their income into retirement (that's $15,000 per year or $1,250 per month) and they averaged a 10% rate of return, which is below the stock market average*, they would have about $1,000,000 in 20 years. And that's if they never got a raise!

---

*The S&P 500 is the most accurate measure of the stock market. The S&P 500 average annual return...

... is 3.55% from 2001 – 2010 (the last 10 years)
... is 11.04% from 1991 – 2010 (the last 20 years)
... is 11.81% from 1971 – 2010 (the last 40 years)
... is 11.95% from 1926 – 2010 (S&P 500's inception)

In 2010, the annual return was 14.32%
In 2009, the annual return was 27.11%
In 2008, the annual return was -37.22%

The stock market is a roller coaster from year-to-year, but if you stay committed for the long haul, it can really pay off!

More important than the number $1,000,000 is what it represents. When you have $1,000,000 in your retirement account and your investment makes a 10% rate of return each year, your retirement account will make $100,000 that year. So, within 20 years, if you invest 15% of your income into retirement, your money will make you more than you make you. Just think, if that same couple stuck with their plan for 40 years, they would have about $8,000,000. That's the power of compound interest working in your favor over time. Most people wait way too long to begin building wealth. *Since you can't go back, the best time to start is right now!*

Year	*Starting Now	*Starting in 20 Years
1	$15,707	
2	$33,059	
3	$52,227	
4	$73,403	
5	$96,796	
6	$122,639	
7	$151,188	
8	$182,726	
9	$217,567	
10	$256,056	
11	$298,576	
12	$345,547	
13	$397,438	
14	$454,762	
15	$518,088	
16	$588,045	
17	$665,328	
18	$750,704	
19	$845,020	
20	$949,211	
21	$1,064,313	$15,707
22	$1,191,467	$33,059
23	$1,331,936	$52,227
24	$1,487,114	$73,403
25	$1,658,542	$96,796
26	$1,847,920	$122,639
27	$2,057,128	$151,188
28	$2,288,243	$182,726
29	$2,543,559	$217,567
30	$2,825,610	$256,056
31	$3,137,195	$298,576
32	$3,481,407	$345,547
33	$3,861,663	$397,438
34	$4,281,737	$454,762
35	$4,745,798	$518,088
36	$5,258,452	$588,045
37	$5,824,787	$665,328
38	$6,450,425	$750,704
39	$7,141,576	$845,020
40	$7,905,099	$949,211
*Investing $1,250 every month at a 10% annual rate of return		

But there's a problem. Most people don't have $1,250 per month left over that they can begin investing and that's because they have payments.

The goal of this book is very simple: if you don't have any payments, you have control of your most powerful wealth-building tool, which is your income. When my wife and I decided to get out of debt forever, we suddenly found the money to begin building wealth. So, the reason I push people into dumping their debt is because I have found a great correlation between becoming debt-free and becoming wealthy.

If you don't have any payments, you have control of your most powerful wealth-building tool, which is your income.

There are tons of books that focus on investing and retirement; this is not one of them. This book is about getting you to do the things that you already know to do that will cause you to reach your dreams and create options in your life.

Sadly, "normal" is living paycheck-to-paycheck, not much money in the bank, hardly any savings for retirement, a marriage hanging on by a thread, stressed out, and carrying quite a bit of debt. Since that's "normal," I don't want to be "normal." I'd rather be "weird."

I am often criticized of being a simpleton – as if I don't understand how money works in the real world – because of the *common sense financial principles* that I spread around. People come up to me and insist that I don't understand how to use debt as a tool or how outdated it is to use cash and a written budget. It used to offend me until I realized where these comments were generally coming from: broke people.

It took me a few years to truly understand that behaviors and habits are a much bigger indicator of how wealthy you will become instead of your education or income level. In his book The Millionaire Next Door, Tom Stanley shares his calculation for how wealthy you should be, based on your age and your income:

$$\text{Expected Net Worth} = \text{Age} * \frac{\text{Current Household Income}}{10}$$

For example, if you are 35-years-old and your household brings in $100,000 per year, your current net worth should be $350,000 [35 * ($100,000/10) = $350,000]. This calculation is a little skewed if you are in your 20s, but still something to shoot for.

Tom Stanley calls the people who have a net worth equal to only half of their expected net worth Under Accumulators of Wealth (UAWs) and people who have a net worth of twice their expected net worth Prodigious Accumulators of Wealth (PAWs). In our example above, a UAW would have a net worth of $175,000 or less [35 * ($100,000/10 * 0.5) = $175,000]. A PAW would have a net worth of $700,000 or more [35 * ($100,000/10 * 2) = $700,000].

Most of our culture falls in the UAW realm; even though many of them have really high incomes. If you're a 50-year-old making $150,000 per year, and you want to be considered a financial success, you should have a net worth of at least $1,500,000

[50 * ($150,000/10) * 2 = $1,500,000]. A typical 50-year-old couple making $150,000 per year who criticizes me of being a simpleton usually has a net worth of about $300,000, which would make them a UAW. Making $150,000 per year implies that they are an intelligent couple, but they should have ended up with more money! It turns out common sense isn't common practice.

Money is About Behavior, Not Math

The most important financial principle that I have learned is that personal finance is more about behavior than math. Dave Ramsey hits the nail on the head when he says, "Personal finance is 80% behavior and only 20% head knowledge." Being a huge math nerd, this concept was a tough pill to swallow.

The fact that money is more about behavior became apparent when I first talked with a young millionaire, who had started with nothing, and I told him how "great" I was doing. This was before I started applying these common sense financial principles of the rich to my life.

> *"Personal finance is 80% behavior and only 20% head knowledge."*
> *-Dave Ramsey*

He started by asking me how my financial situation was going. I told him that it felt like things were going well: we pay everything on time, we have some in savings, and we have a lot of fun. It looked great from the outside. He then asked me how much debt we had. I told him that we had a car payment, but "everybody has a car payment," we have student loan payments, but "that was an investment in our future," and we have a big screen TV payment, but "it was no payments, no interest for one year, so we were beating up the TV company." My finance professor from college would have been so proud.

He then asked me to add up my net worth. You can do this by making a list of all of the big-ticket items you own and a list of all of your debt and subtract the total of your debt from the total of everything you own. He and I did this together; we added up about $17,000 in things we owned and just over $52,000 in debt. Subtracting $52,000 from $17,000 was something that had not crossed my mind prior to that, but it ends up being negative $35,000!

We had been working at great jobs, making great money, and we had nothing to show for it! We made way too much money to be this broke and for our future to not be any brighter than it was. So, in an instant, my world got turned upside down and I stopped telling him how "great" I was doing and I started listening. He didn't have negative money; he had positive money and lots of it. He was obviously doing something I was not. I learned more in that meeting about how money really works than I had in my entire lifetime.

With a new drive to turn my negative into a big positive, I began studying wealthy people like it was my full-time job. Everyone has opinions on money, but I didn't want everyone's opinion. I wanted the opinions of really wealthy people. All of my research has pointed to the fact that before you can get the mathematics of personal finance to work, you need to get your behaviors, attitudes, and habits under control. After all, if I was doing math, I wouldn't be where I was with a negative net worth.

It turns out that academic, mathematical knowledge does not solve personal financial issues. Your behaviors and habits are more of an indicator of becoming wealthy than your academic classroom theory. Even CPAs and professionals with an MBA in finance often have major money problems; many have come to me for guidance.

Most people think more money will solve their problems. That's not true. If I could wave a wand and magically make all of your debt disappear, you're going to be right back in debt again if you don't change your habits.

We didn't have a math problem, we had a behavior problem, and our behaviors were going to have to be modified to win.

After my meeting, I began realizing what was holding me back from winning with money: me. I had found the problem in a place I had never looked, my mirror. I had also found the opportunity, because I had the ability to change it by taking control of my money.

You may have heard that half of solving a problem is realizing that you have one, and it's the truth. How do solve a problem you don't have? You don't. It was difficult for me to do, but to admit out loud that I was the problem with my money was what allowed me to take control of it. My wife and I were about to embark on a process to change our behavior and the results completely transformed our lives.

The Problem

After reading how wealthy people think and what wealthy people do, you're probably going to come to the conclusion that there are no real "secrets of the rich." You'll feel like you already knew most of this information, and you're probably going to be right. You already know what to do, it's the doing it part that's tough. After all, if it was easy, everyone would be wealthy. This book is designed to give you the information and inspiration to take action and take control of your money.

You already know what to do, it's the doing it part that's tough. If it was easy, everyone would be wealthy.

Just like gardening, personal finance is based on cause and effect. You have to intentionally plant, fertilize, till, weed, and care for a garden. When you plant tomatoes, you grow tomatoes, you don't grow cucumbers. What you plant in the ground grows. You reap what you sew.

In his book Outliers, Malcolm Gladwell shows that the world's ultra successful, he calls them outliers, get where they are after a steady accumulation of advantages and extraordinary opportunities that most people never see. Some of the opportunities are as random as the day, month, year, or decade they were born, but all of the outliers had one principle in common: at least 10,000 hours of practice. 10,000 hours is a lot of hard work. It's a lot of intentionally planting, fertilizing, tilling, weeding, and caring for your craft.

Almost everything that happens to you, good and bad, is based on a series of decisions you have made up to that point. If you implement these common sense financial principles into your life, they work regardless of your circumstances.

Think about the idea of cause and effect the next time you hear that someone or some group of people say that they're stuck, they can't get ahead, or they're held back. They spend all of their time giving excuses for not winning. They complain about external factors that cause them to be broke or poor.

People are broke and poor for one of three reasons:

1. Some people don't win the lottery of life and are not born into a great country like America. Instead, they are born in a third world country. Being born in a country like America is a huge opportunity being as the poor in America would be considered rich in most other countries.

2. Some people are oppressed by immoral people that steal money from the poor. Disguised as services to help poor people, payday loans, title pawn shops, cash advances, and the lottery rip people off and damage their lives.

3. Most other people that don't have any money simply have not implemented these common sense financial principles into their lives. This book will help you install these necessary principles and change your life forever.

The Solution

If you're like me, you've heard the rich get richer and the poor get poorer. Like me, you've probably even repeated it. Unlike most financial statements that spread throughout our culture, this one really is true. The rich *do* get richer and the poor *do* get poorer.

There's a reason for this and it's surprisingly simple: **the rich get richer because they do rich people stuff and the poor get poorer because they do poor people stuff**. It's that easy. Rich people apply these common sense financial principles to their lives. There are four distinct paths that you can take with your money:

1. You can start rich and stay rich.
2. You can start rich and become poor.
3. You can start poor and stay poor.
4. You can start poor and become rich.

Most of us do not start off rich, so this gives us two options: staying poor or becoming rich. You have the power to choose which path you will take.

This is not a book that is going to teach you how to get rich quick because get rich quick simply doesn't work in the real world. There is no midnight cable infomercial that can solve your issues. There are no "secrets of the rich" you're missing out on. It's not going to be easy. Winning with money involves sacrifice, but I guarantee that if you start thinking like wealthy people and doing wealthy people things, you will begin to build some serious wealth.

Albert Einstein summed up the ugly truth when he said, **"The definition of insanity is continuing to do the same thing over and over and expecting a different result."** Basically, you're going to have to change. It's going to be a struggle at first. It's going to involve some sacrifices now so that you won't have to sacrifice later. But then and only then, will you begin to win with your money.

Most people need two things when it comes to money. First, most people need to realize that they can do better with money (everyone can do better, but you need to wrap your mind around the idea that *you* can do better). There are three mental obstacles that hold us back from getting the best use of our money. Once you get past these obstacles, getting out of debt and building wealth will be a simple choice. Part 1 of this book will get you past these three obstacles.

Second, most people need to change their attitudes, their behaviors, and their habits around money to do the things that they already know how to do and some of the things they learn to do. Behavior modification is the most important step to winning with money. Once you begin to think like wealthy people, Part 2 of this book will show you step-by-step exactly what actions you need to take to become financially fit.

There are four behaviors that must be modified for you to build a solid financial foundation, and this book addresses all four of them.

1. You need to develop and stick to a monthly budget.
2. You need to get completely out of debt.
3. You need to build a vision for your future by setting goals.
4. You need to implement accountability into your financial plan.

Anybody Can Do This

It doesn't matter if you didn't graduate from high school or if you have an MBA in finance. The principles stay the same. It doesn't matter if you make $40,000 per year, $100,000 per year, or $500,000 per year. The principles stay the same. It doesn't matter if you're single or you're married. The principles stay the same. It doesn't matter if you're 25-years-old, 45-years-old, or 65-years-old. The principles stay the same.

Just because anybody can do this doesn't mean everybody will. In fact, most people will not because you have to have the desire. It has to really be your goal. The drive and the desire is what it really takes and that is a choice you can make starting today.

Wait! If You've Been Paying Attention...

You may have seen the problem. It's the problem that most people see that plagues my entire argument. My argument so far:

1. Normal is "I can't figure out where my money goes," and "I look good on the outside, but I don't have any money."
2. When it comes to finances (or any other area of your life), normal stinks.
3. The problem with my money is not math; it's me, my behavior, my habits, and my attitudes. I already know what to do; I'm just not doing it.
4. There are four things that I can do that will cause me to become financially fit. They are really simple to understand and anyone can do them.

So, you may be wondering if this is so effective, why doesn't everyone do it? *Exactly!*

The Reasons Everyone Doesn't Do It

Most people are so overly confident in their ability to handle their money that they don't pay attention to what they're doing.

People who don't think about their money lose it. It's your responsibility to manage your money, and you're going to lose it if you don't know what's going on.

As you read on, you will uncover the lies and financial myths that have brainwashed our culture and left most people financially flabby.

This book is not designed for people who are in serious financial trouble and can't meet their monthly obligations. It's designed for ordinary people who come to learn that they don't want to be ordinary anymore. They want to be extraordinary.

Your 90 Day Money Challenge

The purpose of the 90 Day Money Challenge is to get you started on your road to financial fitness. After years of financial coaching and counseling, I have discovered that the two biggest deterrents of someone who wants to take control of their money are:

1. Having a crystal clear, step-by-step plan to take you from where you are to where you want to go.
2. Getting started!

This book is designed to help you with both.

The thought of decades of handling money wisely seems to overwhelm most people, so I just want you to try it for 90 days. If you do, you'll see the amazing results and they will keep you going in the right direction. If you find out that I'm wrong after 90 days, you can do something different. What have you got to lose?

Another reason for the 90 days is that it takes a while to change some of your financial habits. As we've discovered, winning with money is about attitudes and actions, not math. You've been handling your money a certain way for so long that it's going to take a few months to implement some new habits into your life. It's similar to the idea of quitting smoking. Some people can quit smoking on the spot if they are told by their doctor that they will die if they continue. Others find excuses for why they can't change, no matter how grave the consequences. Scientific research shows that it takes somewhere between 21 and 40 days to change a habit if you have the desire, and I have found that almost everyone can do it with their finances within 90 days.

If you give this challenge an honest shot for 90 days and you find that it doesn't work, then you can choose to quit. But the uncomfortable truth is if you keep doing what you've been doing, you're going to keep getting what you've been getting, and that's not working. So, if you save some money and pay off debt and you don't like it, you can go blow all your savings and get right back in more debt. You can always go back. But I assure you, if you complete this challenge, you will see more progress in the next 90 days than you have probably seen in the last 90 months.

If you keep doing what you've been doing, you're going to keep getting what you've been getting...

If you're interested in my road to financial fitness, here's the short story. As I mentioned, my wife and I started out our marriage with over $52,000 in debt. We only had about $4,000 in the bank. I always had dreams of being successful, being able to support my family, having my wife be a full-time mom, becoming wealthy one day, sending my kids to school, retiring with dignity, and being able to help so many people through giving, but I had no clear plan about how to get there.

It seemed like things were going great. Then, I started discovering that "normal" in North America is broke and stressful and we were walking down the path that normal people follow. So, I decided I was going to learn how money really works. I was no longer going to take financial advice from normal people because normal people are broke. I started studying wealthy people and learning the principles that caused them to become wealthy.

Then, we started applying these common sense financial principles to our own lives. We were able to agree on our goals and we changed our way of thinking together. We gained control and a sense of our own destiny. We started by selling our $17,000 Toyota 4-Runnder and using $3,000 from our savings to buy a worn out 15-year-old Honda Accord. We developed a written game plan, cut our lifestyle to almost nothing, and got intense. We paid off all of our debt and built an emergency fund of $15,000 in less than one year.

While we were getting out of debt, I began leading Dave Ramsey's Financial Peace University at my church and quickly realized that the reason I am on this planet is to share this material with people and transform their lives. I was personally trained by Dave Ramsey's team in Nashville, Tennessee, to become a Certified Financial Counselor. Since then, I was selected as one of his top three out of 1,500 counselors to present at his follow-up training.

Within months, we had beaten our debt, began building

wealth, and we were free – free to do what we were designed to do. I left my public accounting job at Ernst & Young and started Hamilton Financial Coaching to empower people with a desire for a better future to beat debt, build wealth, and be free. A few years of serving hundreds of families led me to want to spread this message to everyone.

This book forces you through the process that causes you to win with money. The good news is that I have been where you are. I'm not recommending putting you through any torture that I wouldn't go through myself. We worked extra, sold a car, cut up our credit cards, started paying for everything with cash, drastically cut expenses, and skipped vacation the year we were getting out of debt. It wasn't the most fun we've ever had, but it was a short walk across hot coals in the big picture of our lives and it was worth it!

I believe in challenging the status quo, thinking differently, taking an unconventional perspective, personal responsibility, and you reap what you sew. My goal is to inspire and encourage people by spreading this life-changing message. I have found that packaging these common sense financial principles in this simple, step-by-step process causes people to change the way they think about money, which causes them to change the way they manage money. I've also been fortunate for the opportunity to walk with many people on their journey toward financial fitness and hold them accountable.

90 Day Critical Action Step

☐ Find out how well you are doing by creating a Net Worth Statement. Make a list of all of your assets (houses, cars, savings accounts, checking accounts, retirement accounts, non-retirement investments, etc.) and a list of all of your debts (mortgages, car loans, credit cards, bank loans, personal loans, student loans, etc.). Then, subtract your total debt from your total assets. This is your net worth.

PART 1:
THINKING DIFFERENTLY

The process of doing better with *your* money always begins with a **counter-cultural decision**. To change *your* life, *you* must first change the way *you* think. Behind everything *you* do is a thought; every behavior is motivated by a belief; every action is prompted by an attitude. It's time to turn off *your* autopilot, **challenge conventional wisdom**, and replace it with what really works in the real world. **This is not theory**. Change always starts first in *your* mind.

2

HOW YOU WERE BRAINWASHED FROM THE START

Red Cars

We've heard the bad wrap for years: red cars will cost you more in insurance premiums. For years there has been this notion that color plays a significant part in calculating insurance costs and many people believe that red cars cost more to insure. According to the Insurance Information Institute, this is a complete myth. Even I used to believe this myth and I have told other people that red cars cost more to insure. Not anymore.

When it comes to car insurance, a lot of factors matter, but the fact is that insurers have no interest in the color of a car. It doesn't matter if your car is red, green, or purple.

Myth Busting

Myth busting is fun. I wound up doing it by accident: researching wealthy people, I discovered that much of what I thought to be true about handling money was nonsense. Learning the truth behind some of the financial myths is the first mental obstacle that you have to get past to begin getting the best use of your money. I hope that some of the lies behind these myths will make you as angry as they made me.

The idea of a cultural myth, like red cars costing more to insure, is that if you and enough other people repeat the myth often enough, eventually it will become accepted as the truth. And the negative side of this is that the way you think determines the way you feel and the way you feel influences the way you act.

There are four main reasons why we do the things we do:

1. Culturally, because *everyone else* does it that way.
2. Traditionally, because we've always done it that way.
3. Rationally, because it seemed, based on our beliefs, logical.
4. Emotionally, because it just felt right, based on our feelings.

We've become so well-adjusted to our culture that we fit into it without even thinking.

We've become so well-adjusted to our culture that we fit into it without even thinking. What if *everyone else* has it wrong? What if the way we've always done it isn't the best way? What if our logic is flawed? What if our feelings are taking us in the wrong direction? If we keep doing what we've been doing, we're going to keep getting what we've been getting.

You must make some counter-cultural, counter-traditional, counter-rational, and counter-emotional decisions if you want to win with money. If you go with the flow and simply do what *everyone else* does, why would you expect to end up anywhere other than where *everyone else* ends up? If you're not willing to take it one step further than the average person is going to, then you're going to end up financially average and mediocre. You need to build principles and habits into your life based on truth. Before we can work on the habits, we need to take a closer look at the truth.

The Brainwashing of America

Have you ever seen the computer game, Lemmings? When it came out in the early 1990s, it was one of the most popular games. The behavior of the creatures in Lemmings is based on the supposed behavior of real lemmings, which are a type of small rodent. Lemmings are believed to go on migrations in mass that eventually lead to disaster; they often choose to cross a body of water that is so wide that it stretches their physical capabilities to the limit, and they drown. They appear to be lacking the common sense to stop and think about why they are doing what they are doing.

Our culture is full of people that resemble these lemmings. We tend to do what *everyone else* is doing. We go along with popular opinion without asking why, and conforming to the norm has potentially dangerous or fatal consequences. The biggest popular opinion that we carry around with us is that debt is a tool that should be used to create prosperity. This is the biggest lie we've been sold. And most of us commit mass financial suicide when we buy into this flawed logic.

Now I know this message sounds weird, but it's also weird to be wealthy. And fighting against the stream of lemmings, our culture, is an uphill battle. Keep an open mind as we unpack the defective logic because **in order to change the way you do things, you need to change the way you look at things**. And the way you change how you look at things is with new information and that is what you're about to pass through your brain.

Myth: You Need to Build Your Credit

The biggest debt lie that you and I have been sold is that you need to build your credit. There are "financial gurus" on television that say a single number, your credit score, is your key to your financial future. You've heard this, and if you're like me, you've probably even said this. I used to be brainwashed myself. Before you just follow what *everyone else* does, let's look at what the credit score is.

Your credit score is often referred to as your FICO score. FICO stands for Fair Isaac Corporation and it's the company that developed the credit score. FICO computes your score and it usually ranges from 300 to 850. On the FICO website, they show you how they calculate your score:

- 35% Debt History.
- 30% Debt Levels.
- 15% Length of Debt History.
- 10% Types of Debt Used.
- 10% New Debt.

Does anything stand out to you when you look at this breakdown? It looks like all 100% of your score is based on your reputation with debt. Exactly! 100% of your credit score is based on your interaction with debt. Do you see anywhere in there anything that has to do with money? No!

The FICO score is not a measure of winning with money. It has nothing to do with it! If you got a raise and doubled your income, do you know what that would do to your FICO score? Nothing! If I gave you $1,000,000, do you know what that would do to your FICO score? Nothing! Again, it has nothing to do with winning with money. It just looks at debt.

> *The FICO score is not a measure of winning with money.*

When you break down the mathematics, the way you drive your credit score up is to do the following:

- 35% - pay all of your debt on time every month.
- 30% - don't have too much debt, but don't have too little because both cause your score do go down.
- 15% - the longer you are in debt, the better.
- 10% - the more types of debt you use, the better.
- 10% - continually borrow money.

To raise your FICO score, you need to go into debt, early and often. Borrow enough money, but not too much money. You can't own anything, you have to have lots of different types of debt, like a mortgage, and a car payment, and a credit card payment, and student loan payments, etc. – you need to have a lot of payments and pay them all on time. I'm all about paying all of your bills on time; it's the rest that I have an issue with.

If you play the bank's game and raise your FICO score so it's really high, what do you get? A higher credit score allows you to borrow more money! So, the logic is to borrow early and often so you can borrow more later on. This is exactly the opposite, as we're about to uncover, of what wealthy people really do. But it's a lie that we've bought and used to run our lives and it's causing us to commit mass financial suicide.

A high credit score is not an indicator that you're wealthy. I would suggest you don't use the credit score as your measure of winning with money. I would use money as your measure. It's hard to build a credit score and wealth at the same time. If after reading and digesting this idea you still have a long-term goal to build and maintain your FICO score, you should question your goal. Your goal with money should be to have some!

Your goal with money should be to have some!

Also, some of the "financial gurus" on television that tell you to do whatever it takes to build your FICO score get paid directly and indirectly by FICO. For example, Suze Orman tells you that your FICO score is the key to your financial future. In his award-winning documentary and book <u>Maxed Out</u>, James Scurlock points out that Suze has a deal with FICO's parent company. Also, Suze has been permitted by FICO to sell a FICO "kit" on her website. Do you think she is making any money off of that? Talk about being biased.

By the way, my FICO score has gone down about 50 points since I stopped borrowing money. I couldn't care less; I don't need a high FICO score because I don't borrow money!

Myth: You'll Always Have a Car Payment

Another lie that you and I have been sold is that you'll always have a car payment. Have you heard that? I have. Have you said that? I used to. **Car payments are the mantra of the middle class**. It's the biggest thing that keeps people broke their entire lives.

Let's look at the math for a minute. The average car payment in America right now is just under $500 per month on a six-year car loan, or 72 months. So, over a 40 year car payment lifetime, the average person has at least one car payment the entire time and gets six or seven cars. If you keep a car payment those 40 years (and it never goes up), you will end up with six or seven rust buckets and about $0 in retirement, like most people. If, on the other hand, you get completely out of debt and start buying cars with cash, which gets really easy when you take control of your money, you won't have any car payments. If you invested that $500 per month in your retirement account for 40 years and you averaged a 10% rate of return, you would end up with over $3,000,000! You would retire wealthy just on what you pay in car payments.

Now, I'm not against you getting nice cars, I'm just against nice cars getting you. Broke people tend to have car payments for most of their lives. Wealthy people don't have car payments, and they didn't get out of car debt when they got wealthy, they got wealthy when they got out of car debt.

I'm not against you getting nice cars, I'm just against nice cars getting you.

Myth: You Need Debt to Get Ahead

The best way to become prosperous is to avoid debt. If you're going to avoid debt, you don't need a FICO score. The wealthiest people never have car payments or credit card payments or student loan payments.

Debt is not a privilege, it's a product. It's a product that banks sell and they are very good at selling it. We've been brainwashed to buy now and pay later because we're impulsive as a society. We want instant gratification, even if it's at the expense of long-term success.

As our culture is full of lemmings, when you start to take control of your money, you will be going against the grain and you're going to get some criticism. The bottom line is when broke people, which is most people, are making fun of your financial plan, you know you're right on track.

Also, good people wouldn't intentionally give you bad advice on purpose. So, just because someone you care about has a different opinion, don't let them convince you to be a lemming. Just understand that you now have a fundamental belief system difference, which means the loved one is not a bad person, they're just uninformed.

Some people that give this bad advice have letters and licenses after their names that make them sound like they know what they're talking about. Letters and licenses after your name doesn't mean you know the correct information, it usually just means you passed the exam that tested your knowledge of what other lemmings do. I've worked with tons of broke financial planners, CPAs, and finance professors. If these teachers and professionals had it all figured out, don't you think they would all be doing great with their money? Well, they're not.

In our lifetimes, the way it was always done was with a car payment, or student loans, or credit cards. The way it was always done was with building your credit. You have got to stop doing it the way it has always been done if you expect to get different results.

As a disclaimer, the only kind of debt that I don't yell about is a mortgage on your first house or the house you are currently in, but you also need a plan to pay that off, and not the normal 30-year plan like most people. The reason I don't yell at this debt is you have to live somewhere and if you don't have the money to pay cash for a house yet, your options are renting or getting a mortgage. But this logic can not be used for car payments, because your options for transportation are not limited to renting a car or financing one. I'm perfectly fine with driving a beater that you pay cash for and then you take what would normally be a car payment and you save it for a few months and you buy a nicer car. This logic can also not be used for college. What?! That's right. You need to pay for your education, and if you want to help your kids through college, you can't borrow money for their education either.

Most people don't do this and most people are broke. Don't do what most people do. Be willing to sacrifice in the short-term to win in the long-term and completely change your life, the lives of your family, and the lives of everyone around you.

If you're renting now and wondering how you can qualify for a mortgage with a good interest rate without a FICO score, you do that through a process called manual underwriting. Basically, it's where a banker spends about 15 minutes looking at your financial situation on paper instead of 15 seconds looking at your FICO score. It's the only way mortgage lending used to be done before the FICO score was introduced, and only about half of the banks still do this. Some banks don't because it "takes too long." That mentality resulted in a bunch of broke people being allowed to buy houses they couldn't afford because they had a high FICO score, which led to many foreclosures in the last decade. You will qualify for the best interest rate under manual underwriting if you meet the following four criteria:

1. Have a steady income in the same industry for at least 12 months.
2. Have paid your rent on time for at least 12 months.
3. Have a reasonable down payment (preferably 20%).
4. Have at least four recurring monthly bills that you have paid on time for at least 12 months, such as cable, cell phone, electricity, and water.

This should not sound too overwhelming. If you don't already own a house, you shouldn't buy one unless you meet these criteria whether or not you have a high FICO score.

Myth: Don't Lose Your Biggest Tax Deduction

Another lie that we have been sold is if I pay off my house, I will lose my only tax deduction. Even CPAs sometimes suggest not paying off your house so you can keep your tax deduction and they're wrong.

Let's look at what a tax deduction does. If you have a $200,000 mortgage at 5% interest, the interest you will pay this year will be about 5% of $200,000, or $10,000. That's how much interest you send to the bank and you are allowed to deduct that $10,000 from your income on your taxes. If you are married and your taxable household income is $100,000, you would be in the 25% tax bracket. So, if you got a $10,000 tax deduction for paying the bank $10,000 in interest, you would not be taxed on $100,000, you would be taxed on $90,000. And if you did this counter-cultural thing I suggest and paid off your house, you would eventually no longer have the $10,000 tax deduction, and you would pay taxes on $100,000 instead of $90,000, a $10,000 difference. Being in the 25% tax bracket, taxes on that extra $10,000 would be $2,500. That's how much more you would have to send Washington, D.C. I know that the thought of paying more in taxes is dreadful, but you wouldn't have to send the bank $10,000. Overall, you

Keeping a mortgage for the tax deduction is just bad math.

would be $7,500 better off! Every time you do something for the tax deduction, you are trading $10,000 for $2,500, or trading dollars for quarters. Keeping a mortgage for the tax deduction is just bad math.

Mortgage Balance	*Mortgage Interest Per Year	Tax Deduction	**Saved on Taxes	Wasted Money
$200,000	$10,000	$10,000	$2,500	$7,500
$0	$0	$0	$0	$0
*Assuming a 5% interest rate		**Assuming a 25% tax bracket		

You can get the exact same tax deduction by giving $10,000 to charity, but you don't hear CPAs telling everyone to do that, do you? No. Paying off your house is a wonderful idea.

Can you imagine how free you would feel if you had no payments in the world, not even a house payment? Do you know how much money you would need to live on each month with no payments? Almost nothing. Having a paid-for house is not normal; neither is being wealthy. Don't let tax deductions hold you back from doing what is right. Now if the tax deduction is there, take it. I'm not against tax deductions; I'm just against bad financial decisions for the sole purpose of getting a tax deduction.

Where You Are Today

What you have falsely believed and acted on or not acted on has brought you to where you are today. If you like where you are, keep doing what you are doing. But if you want to be in a better place, you need to believe and do different things.

3

TWO ATTITUDES THAT DESTROY WEALTH

Fighting Words

Besides buying into the lies that our culture has sold, there are two attitudes that will destroy your ability to build wealth: **denial** and **ignorance**. Those are fighting words to most people. Don't get defensive about it. I'm not picking on you; I'm picking on ideas that we all, including myself, carry around.

Being in denial that we could be doing better with handling our money is the second mental obstacle that holds us back from getting the best use of our money. Denial causes us to not pay attention like we should. Once we begin paying attention, a third mental obstacle, ignorance, causes us to become overwhelmed because we don't know where we should start. This decision paralysis leads to a lack of hope, which will destroy your chances of success.

Denial

Denial is an unconscious defense mechanism that we keep in our head to reduce anxiety. If we don't think about it and admit we could do better, it's not a problem. Sometimes we think we are doing so well because we look like Ken and Barbie on the outside; we drive nice cars and live in nice houses. When this happens, we're unwilling to acknowledge that we can do better and that causes us to not search for a better way. We want others to think we have everything under control. Until you wrap your mind around the idea that no matter where you are, everyone can do better, you won't pay attention to what you are doing and change where you are going.

Paying Attention

Money flows from people who don't pay attention to how they handle it, to people who do. You've got to change the way you look at money because you can't half pay attention. You can't fake it. You can't walk along and act like everything is okay. You have to be very intentional about your steps, what you're doing, where you are, where you want to go, and how you're going to get there. When you don't pay attention, mediocrity starts to sneak up on you.

> *Money flows from people who don't pay attention to how they handle it, to people who do.*

Do you remember your first job when you got your first paycheck? You probably didn't have many expenses at the time, if any, and it was fun. The paycheck may not have been huge, but it was yours. When was the last time your payday was that fun? It's probably been a while because slowly over time, your expenses rose faster than your income and now most people go to work just to pay bills.

Sadly, by most people's standards, financial mediocrity is okay. Let's see what mediocre looks like.

Normal in North America

To sum it up, normal is broke or one emergency away from being there:

- 70% of Americans are living paycheck-to-paycheck.
- 68% of Americans could not cover a $5,000 emergency without going into debt.
- 49% of families could not cover even one month's expenses if they were to miss a paycheck.
- 53% of Americans have less than $25,000 in retirement savings. 43% of those people are over 55.
- 83% of adults age 20 – 49 say their current financial situation is very or somewhat stressful.
- 52% of the marriages in America end in divorce, and of those that divorce in the first seven years, 90% of them say money problems caused it.
- Due to a lack of savings, 60% of the 77,000,000 baby boomers will not have the means to support their current standard of living when the reach retirement.

If any of this sounds like your situation, you're not alone. You may feel like you are. You may feel like you've done things no one else would ever do, but you're not alone. You're in the majority, with seven out of ten people. The point of these scary statistics is not to make you feel better about your situation. It's to show you that normal is broke or on the edge of broke and hopefully it causes you to not want to be normal.

If you truly are in the three out of ten people that are doing better than this – you don't have any payments and you could easily cover a $5,000 emergency without having to go into debt – you can still do better, and you need to. **Everyone can do better, even the guy writing this book**. There are about 8,000,000 people in North America today that are millionaires – that's only about 2.5% of the population. It's so simple to get there, but so few people actually do.

We are all familiar with the heightened reaction we feel when we've narrowly avoided a traffic accident because we aren't paying attention while we are driving. If you don't pay attention while you are driving, eventually you will crash. The same thing happens with our money. You have to pay attention if you want to win with money. You have to acknowledge you can do better. The behaviors in Part 2 of this book will take you from your current financial situation to a much better place.

Ignorance

If someone calls you ignorant, all those primitive reflexes start kicking in, from the sweaty palms and goose bumps, to the quivering tense muscles and shortness of breath. Before you dive head first into the fight or flight response, let's redefine ignorance. Ignorance is not a lack of intelligence; ignorance is a lack of know-how.

Picture in your mind right now the cockpit of a huge airplane. It has two steering wheels that move in all directions, about eight digital screens, and about 10,000 instruments, switches, and lights. Now picture yourself in the pilot's chair and no one else around. Do you think you could fly the plane across the country and land safely without any help? I'm betting you can't. That makes you ignorant. You can't fly a plane. It doesn't mean you're not intelligent, it just means you don't have that particular skill.

Handling Money is a Learned Skill

No one looks at a newborn baby and says, "This baby is a financial genius." We are not born with the skills required to handle money; they must be learned.

That leads to another problem with our money. No one really teaches us how to handle money well. They don't teach it in high school or college. Most parents don't teach it, or they try to teach it, but they are in the normal crowd who are not getting the best use of their

Taking financial advice from broke people is like taking diet and exercise advice from fat people.

money. Taking financial advice from broke people is like taking diet and exercise advice from fat people. Over 60% of Americans are overweight or obese. These are not the people we should ask for help when we are trying to get physically fit. Similarly, broke people are not who we should ask when we are trying to get financially fit.

Along the way, we do pick up some good ideas from all over, but not many people have it all together. We hear people say it's a good idea to invest in retirement, it's a good idea to save money, it's a good idea to get out of debt, it's a good idea to… [you fill in the blank]. Although most of these ideas are good, there are so many things we could do with our money. For most people, having to choose from all of these options causes decision paralysis, and they become overwhelmed, which causes them to not do anything. They get paralyzed. When you become overwhelmed, you freeze, like a deer in the headlights.

I have found that any time I am facing too big a decision, what I've got to do is break down the decision into parts that I can swallow and then prioritize the parts. That's how you eat an elephant, one bite at a time. And your personal finances are an elephant, because there are too many moving parts. So, while all those things are important, they still need to be executed in a specific order that will cause you to lay a solid financial foundation.

It's like building a house. The roof is very important, but it really doesn't matter until the foundation is right. The lumber package really doesn't matter if it's sitting on a crummy foundation. So, you should build your finances in order, step-by-step, taking you from where you are to where you want to go, one step at a time.

You're a smart person. If an opportunity came your way to make a one time lump sum of $10,000,000 if you could figure out how to fly a large airplane, would you go figure out how to do it? Sure you would. You would identify the problem and go solve the problem by gaining knowledge from people who can actually fly.

In personal finance, you need new tools, skills, and knowledge as well. You will find these tools in Part 2 of this book, and you need to begin using them!

In chapter 6, you will begin setting goals and building a vision for your future. I will help you layout a proven, step-by-step process that will cause you to beat debt and build wealth in the fastest and most effective way. When you develop a game plan to get what you want, you will start to develop the belief that you can get it, and that belief leads to hope.

Hope

Hope is when you believe that what you are doing is going to bring the desired result, and hope is a powerful thing. When you don't have hope, you're paralyzed. When you don't have hope and you don't believe the results of your actions are going to cause you to win in any area of your life, then you don't do those actions. You experience hopelessness when you give up.

I have discovered that injecting hope into your finances through building a long range plan, or a vision of where you are going, is as important as having a plan. The vision doesn't matter unless there's hope. It doesn't matter unless it takes you to where you need to go with your money, with your family, and with your future. Hope is what causes you to sacrifice some things now so you can send the kids to college, truly own a home, and retire with dignity.

Building a vision is necessary for your dreams to come true. Dreams need to become a vision for the future. Out of that vision will flow goals, and out of your goals will flow the daily activities that it takes to accomplish your goals that cause your vision to come into view. Then, you will wake up one day and live your dreams.

It's time to turn your dreams into reality. It's time to replace any stress that you have with hope by seeing a light at the end of the tunnel that's not an oncoming train. The vision is the catalyst. It's the one thing that will spring you into action towards your goals.

Starting the Journey

Getting started with your 90 Day Money Challenge may not be the most fun you've ever had, that's why it's really important to have a vision for your future. When we were getting out of debt, the only thing that got my wife and I through that period of time was looking past the debt and telling ourselves where we were going was worth it. **The only way to get through a mess and not smell it is to look past it**. The things you go through and the sacrifices make it hard. The only good thing involved is what it's going to feel like when you get there. When you can walk out your front door, breathe in the air, and not owe a sole in the world; that's going to be worth it!

It's now time for you to choose what you are going to do. We've uncovered the lies and obstacles that prevent people from getting the best use of their money. You're already farther along in the financial literacy journey than most people will ever be. But now you have to choose between two paths. You can continue to do what you have been doing and continue getting the results you have been getting. Or, you can start doing what wealthy people do. I challenge you to try this out for 90 days. If you don't like it after 90 days, you can always go back.

Now let's turn to see exactly what you need to do to start winning with you money.

PART 2:
ACTING DIFFERENTLY

The way *you* think determines the way *you* feel and the way *you* feel influences the way *you* act. **The truth must become the compass that *you* rely on** for *your* direction, not culture, tradition, or emotion. Developing new habits based on what wealthy people do will cause *you* to become wealthy. Whether or not this material will **change *your* life for the better** is not in question; the only question that remains is **will *you* do it?**

4
HOW TO SUCCEED WITH YOUR MONTHLY BUDGET

You, Inc.

There was a question that Dave Ramsey asked me a while ago and it shook me up so bad, it changed my life. He asked, "If you managed money for a company called You, Inc., the way you manage money for you now, would you fire you?" To be honest with myself, I had to answer yes. And it was really frustrating. From the outside, things looked great, but I didn't really have anything to show for it. I made too much money to not know where it was going.

I found out that there was only one way to fix that. I learned that I had to start paying attention and being very proactive with my money. It was a breakthrough to understand that you can not make enough to out-earn your stupidity. I had been trying it for years. No one can successfully do that for an extended period of time.

If I paid you $10,000 to manage money for someone who makes $50,000 per year, what would be the first thing you would do?

You would make him write it down. As of today, you are in charge of finances for You, Inc., and I have a job that could be worth way more than $10,000 for you if you do it correctly. It could be worth millions! Because that's about what it's worth to you if you start saving and investing now.

After my wife and I turned our financial lives around and I started helping others, it was weird to me that I would find people making $50,000 per year who had a pile of money and people making $150,000 per year who had a pile of debt. I kept asking myself mathematically, how can that be, and it had to do with who was making their money behave.

In this chapter, we are going to unpack the process where you will learn to start being very intentional with your money and make it behave.

This is Not Your Normal Budget

Most people don't know what a real budget is or how much it can help them. Most people think a budget is when they simply write down about seven expenses that they have to pay for each month. Boy is that wrong. In this chapter, we are going to redefine what a budget is, but first, let's explore the common causes of why most people don't do a budget:

- It sounds like you can never have any fun.
- It has been used to abuse a spouse.
- Many people are afraid of what they will see if they actually write down what they are spending.
- Most people have never had a budget that worked.

There are many of reasons most budgets don't work and this chapter is designed to fix these problems.

Budgets don't work when:

- You leave things out.
- You overcomplicate your plan.
- You base everything on the average month.
- You don't write it down.
- You don't actually live like it says.

So, if most people don't do a budget and most budgets don't work, why would doing a budget help? Before a budget will help, you have to understand what a real budget is, not what *everyone else* thinks it is.

The way you need to look at a budget is, "I'm telling my money what to do this month, before the month begins, instead of wondering where it went." That's all it is!

Unfortunately, the word budget has gotten a bum rap – it is basically just a plan. When you budget, you're spending on paper, on purpose, before the month begins. But many people view a budget as a straight jacket that keeps them constrained. "Freedom" and "budget" just don't seem to go together. However, when you see that a budget is just spending your money with intention, you'll actually experience more freedom than before.

Accounting programs like Quicken do not take the place of budgeting. What those programs do is look backward on what happened in the past, not what is going to happen in the future. Quicken works like the hit TV show *CSI*: you can find out how the patient died by looking at the evidence, but it doesn't prevent the patient from dying. Using an accounting program as your guide is like trying to drive a car by only looking at the rear view mirror. It doesn't work.

Why You Should Do a Monthly Budget

There are many reasons you should do a budget, and here are some of them. You will be amazed by how powerful it can be. We've been talking about how you need to pay attention to your money, and the monthly budget is the way you pay attention.

You will surprise yourself because you will feel like you got a raise. Managed money goes farther. To the untrained person, it sounds so disciplined, controlling, and pushy, and yet it relieves a lot of stress. If you're married, a budget will remove many fights from your marriage. When you make your money behave, it truly changes your life.

You will feel more secure knowing that you are taking care of your family whether or not life works according to plan when you add the right components to your budget. Writing your plan down will show where you are doing good and it will point out any gaps that you need to fill in.

You will be empowered because you will be in control - telling your money where to go instead of wondering where it went. The budget is going to show if you are overspending in an area, and you are the one who gets to decide if you are overspending, not anyone else. Also, you will gain a sense of hope as you begin setting and achieving your goals.

Step-By-Step Plan to Put Together Your Monthly Budget

Now that you're ready to take control of your money, let's lay out the ground rules for doing a budget that really works.

Your budget needs to be written. It can be written on paper or on the computer. The first step is to write down what is actually happening.

Your budget needs to be planned for this coming month, not the average month. There's never an average month.

At the top of the page, list the income that you know is coming in this month. Add up all of the income lines for the month. If you do not have a regular  income that you can plan on, make your best guess at what your income will be for this month. If it can range from a low to a high income, use a conservatively low estimate.

www.
Download the Budget Form!

Below the total income line, list all of your monthly expenses for this month and the amount you plan on paying.

Some expenses are easy to list because they occur every single month, such as rent/mortgage, electricity, cell phone, cable, and NetFlix. Auto pay these expenses as much as possible. For any debts besides the house, such as car payments, credit card payments, or student loan payments, list the amount you normally pay.

Some expenses are a little more difficult to list because they do not occur every single month, such as car insurance, life insurance, and a quarterly water bill. Although these are more difficult to predict, this step is necessary. Determine how much you need to save each month for a planned expense. If you have four months to save for a $400 car insurance payment, set aside $100 per month in the budget. When you get past the four months, if you have six months to save for a $400 car insurance payment, set aside $75 per month in the budget. Transfer this savings amount from your checking account to a separate savings account for each item in this list at the end of every single month. Then, when it comes time to pay that bill, use the money in this account to pay it.

Some expenses are much more difficult to list because they are not every month and they don't have specific amounts, such as gifts, Christmas, kids' activities, sports, car maintenance, and vacation. Do a side budget for these expenses by choosing how much you are going to spend on each item and dividing that amount by the amount of time you have until it's time to pay for it. Just like the non-monthly expenses above, transfer this savings amount at the end of every single month and use the money in this account when it's time to pay for the item.

Don't forget other common expenses such as groceries, gas for the cars, doctor co-pays, prescriptions, entertainment, clothes, and eating out.

Now that you have a planned amount to pay or save for all of your expenses, add up all of the expense lines for the month.

At the bottom of the page, add a category called disposable income and fill in this amount by taking your total income line and subtracting your total expenses line.

If this number is negative, we have a problem because this number is not allowed to be negative. **You can not spend more than you make, you're not in Congress!** If this number is negative, you have to adjust the income (bring in more money) or the expenses (spend or save less money) to cause this disposable income number to be positive.

When, not if, the disposable income number is positive, it's time to start telling your money what to do. A real budget should be a zero-based budget where every dollar of your income should be allocated to some category and the disposable income line (total income minus total expenses) equals exactly zero. You will eventually allocate every dollar of this disposable income line to other expense lines in your budget. I suggest that you don't allocate this money for anything until you read chapter 6.

Congratulations, you now have a real budget for next month where you are telling your money where to go before the month even begins. When you do this properly, you're probably going to have a pile left over and you're going to want to kick yourself for not doing this earlier. Don't get too upset at the past. You can't go back. I want you to learn from what happened, but focus on moving forward.

The Budget Committee Meeting

If you're married, it's time for the Budget Committee Meeting (BCM). The BCM is a quick meeting you should have with your spouse before every month for the rest of your lives. It's designed to unify your plan with your spouse where you both have an equal vote. In your marriage, you need to make a decision together that you are both going to handle money together each and every month for the rest of your lives. You are not taking over the money, your spouse is not taking over the money, you are going to work together and you both have a vote. You are both adults. You're not daddy taking care of a spoiled little girl or mommy taking care of a little boy and dishing out his allowance; you are two adults working together.

Most marriages have two sets of differences. Whoever said opposites attract hit the nail on the head. First, one of you is a nerd and one of you is a free spirit. The term nerd does not mean controlling. Nerd means that you are very detail driven. Nerds usually have a spreadsheet for everything and could roll around in numbers all day. The term free spirit doesn't mean irresponsible or immature. Free spirit means that you're just not wired in such a way that details are the love of your life. Free spirits would rather be outside than be working on a spreadsheet.

Second, one of you is a spender and one of you is a saver. Being a spender isn't a bad thing; spenders help you have a life. Being a saver isn't a bad thing either; savers help by keeping the spender from doing something when you can't afford to do it. With all of these differences, there is a silver lining: you need each other. Neither one of you is right or wrong; it's just how you're wired. You don't need to change personalities, just attitudes and habits.

Now that we know you have these differences, it's time to set some ground rules for this meeting.

This meeting should take place at the kitchen table with the TV off.

The nerd should put the budget together and bring it to the meeting. Now it's time for the nerd to be quiet. All of your opinions are on the page; you don't need to say anything until the free spirit has a question. Lastly, the nerd has to let the free spirit change something. I know this freaks you out, but you're getting their support when you make it "our" plan. You need to compromise with the free spirit. In this meeting, you're working together emotionally to plan your ideas of a better life through teamwork.

The free spirit has rules as well. They must come to the meeting. They must talk at the meeting and have mature input. They must agree to every number on the page or they have to vote to change it. Lastly, they can't say "whatever you want to do." This is part of having mature input.

Once both of you agree on the budget, it's now a contract for the month. Treat this meeting as a contract that you are both going to stick to spending the amounts you agreed to at the meeting. Pinky swear and spit shake that you will stick to it. The BCM is the biggest thing that can improve your marriage and stop money fights, assuming you can keep your word

> *The BCM is the biggest thing that can improve your marriage and stop money fights.*

and you have integrity. Make each other a promise and keep that promise.

If this is the first time you have done a budget with this much detail, I can almost guarantee the first month is not going to work out according to plan. It's not going to work perfectly, but it does get easier. When something comes up that wasn't planned, it's time for an Emergency BCM. If you have to add an expense to the budget or change an amount, that's fine, but you have to rebalance it. Then change the future budgets if it's going to happen again. Hint: Christmas is in December this year! "Unexpected events" like these are where most people throw out the budget and think it doesn't work. Another hint: The car is going to break, so you should save for car maintenance.

This first meeting you have should take about 30-minutes. The second should be about 20-minutes. After that, they don't need to be any longer than 10-minutes.

It's okay if it doesn't work out perfectly the first time. Changing habits is hard work at first, but it gets easier as you go. For example, research shows that people who quit the very addictive smoking habit take five, six, or seven tries before they finally quit for good. Yet, smokers are surprised that they can't quit on the first or second try. The budget works the same way. Anticipate a few setbacks the first few months and know they will begin to go away after you fine tune and adjust for 90 days.

If you're having trouble getting your spouse on board, here are two things that can help. First, you may be talking too much about *what* you want to do and not enough about the *why* you want to do it. Chances are that both of you want the same big goals. Talk about *how it would feel* to… [insert something your spouse would really look forward to]. Come up with a goal that is bigger than yourself (being financially independent, taking care of others, a huge vacation every year, etc.). If you've already screwed up and only talked about the *what*, you need to apologize. Second, start using words like "we" and "our," not "you" or "I" when you are talking about your finances or dreams. Use phrases like "we are going to do a budget" and "we are going to work together."

Now that you can agree on what you're spending, it's time to make sure you are completely on the same page. What I'm prescribing is going to be very uncomfortable if you're not already doing it, but what you're doing isn't working as well as it should be, so you need to change it. I'm going to propose that you unify and have one checking account and you have one written budget that you both have a vote on. You both agree to it before the month begins, and no money is spent unless it's written on the page. Then you can operate with one checking account without bouncing checks.

It's going to be a very uncomfortable 90 days. Give each other grace and be gentle the first three months you do this. You're going to learn to work together in a way you've never worked together before and you're going to see your marriage improve dramatically.

Discipline

Now that you are agreeing on your plan and you are operating out of the same account, it's time to live like the page shows. Most people that layout a budget get to the end of the month and they go over in a lot of categories and go under in a few categories. Most people think sticking to the budget is really hard to do because things come up. Actually, it doesn't have to be that hard. Most of the expenses in your budget are predictable, like bills. There are a few categories that can cause big problems though, and for those I insist you use cash.

Cash builds instant discipline into your plan. Before you break your plan, you will run out of cash and you can change your budget on purpose and rebalance it before you get yourself into trouble. In his book The Millionaire Mind, Tom Stanley outlines the character qualities of the wealthiest people in America. Here is his list of the top 10:

1. Be honest with all people. (tied for #1)
1. Being well disciplined. (tied for #1)
3. Getting along with people.
4. Having a supportive spouse.
5. Working harder than most people.
6. Loving my career/business.
7. Having strong leadership qualities.
8. Having a very competitive spirit/personality.
9. Being very well organized.
10. Having an ability to sell my ideas/products.

You'll notice that there is not one mathematical quality on this list (actually the first mathematical quality is #11, making wise investments). These are the ten things that the wealthiest people in America would tell you if you asked them what it took to be wealthy. These are not normal people. These are rich people and if you want to be rich people, you need to do what rich people do. By the way, eight out of ten of these millionaires and billionaires are first generation rich. Getting on a budget, or being very well organized, is #9 on his list. More important than having a budget is actually sticking to it by being well disciplined. It's tied for the #1 most important quality of becoming wealthy.

If you want to be rich people, you need to do what rich people do.

The best way to be disciplined with your new budget is to

put yourself in an environment that makes discipline easy, and the best way to do that is to use the envelope system. For a few categories in your budget, take the amount that you are willing to spend out of the bank at the beginning of the month and then when you spend money in those categories, use that cash. For example, if you are planning on spending $500 per month on groceries, take the $500 out of the bank in cash at the beginning of the month and put in an envelope labeled "Groceries." When it comes time to go to the grocery store, take the grocery cash with you, and when the money runs out, stop buying groceries! If you decide you don't like the number, it's okay to take out more money after you change and re-balance the budget. This will ensure that you do not overspend and blow your budget. The categories you should try this with for the first 90 days are all of the categories where you spend money outside of the house for "food" and "fun" (groceries, eating out, clothes, and entertainment).

When my wife and I started doing everything in this book, it was very uncomfortable. We had just had our first BCM and my wife thought this process was just going to be another quick phase of mine (after all, it was only about a month before we started this that I had asked her to put every single purchase, no matter how big or small it was, on our credit card to get the reward points). We had committed to using cash for groceries, eating out, clothes, and entertainment.

Excited to get control of our money, I was the one who volunteered to go to the bank and get all of the cash for the month. Then we went on our first big grocery store trip. I don't normally go to the grocery store, but I was so fired up about being on the same page with money, I was excited to go. When we went to check out with our overflowing cart of groceries, I realized that I had forgotten the grocery cash at home. What an idiot I was! This is where my wife and I had our last money disagreement, right there in the only open non-self-checkout lane in the Super Fresh grocery store. We had enough money in the checking account to pay with our debit card, but I didn't want to do that because we had committed to using cash. So, I wanted to go home and get the cash. My wife just wanted to pay with our debit card and put the cash back in the bank, which would have saved a trip home, a lot of time, and all the gas to get back and forth to the store again.

It was not a fun ride home. Or a fun ride back to the store. Or a fun ride back home again. Or fun putting the groceries away. Or a fun weekend. But that is the point where my wife will tell you, many years later, it clicked for her. That is the point where hope was built. We were really doing this. This wasn't a theory. We were really going to finally take control of our money. Being very well disciplined is critical, especially in the first 90 days of starting this challenge.

Give the envelope system an honest try for 90 days, and then if you don't like it, you can stop. But what you will find if you give it an honest try is that you will start achieving the goals that you layout later in the book and it will be due to getting organized with a budget and staying disciplined to your plan. Try it!

90 Day Critical Action Steps

☐ Create a written budget for this month, not the average month. This can be on paper or on the computer. If you don't know how much you are going to spend in a category, make your best guess.

☐ The budget must include all of your spending, saving, and giving that you plan on doing for this month.

☐ The budget has to balance. The income at the top must equal the expenses going down the page. If there is any leftover money, you have to add a category, preferably money to use towards your next long range goal from chapter 6, and tell it where to go.

☐ If you're married, you need to agree on the budget with your spouse before you begin spending any more money.

☐ If the month has already started, write down what you have already spent for each category.

☐ Keep track of all of your expenses for each category.

☐ Pick at least one category to try the cash envelope system.

☐ Stick to your budget. This gets easier and easier over the first 90 days.

☐ After the 1st month is over, create a budget for the 2nd month. By keeping track of what you actually spend in the 1st month, creating the budget for the 2nd month should be a lot easier.

☐ After the 2nd month is over, create a budget for the 3rd month. By keeping track of what you actually spend in the 2nd month, creating the budget for the 3rd month should be a lot easier.

☐ Create a budget every single month for the rest of your life.

This will become a habit after a few months and once it is a habit, it will be very easy to do.

5

HOW TO GET COMPLETELY OUT OF DEBT FOREVER

The Wealthiest People in America

In studying wealthy people, I came across a study about the Forbes 400. Forbes Magazine ranks the 400 wealthiest Americans every year and publishes them in a special edition of their magazine called the Forbes 400. Out of these 400 people, somewhere between 80% and 90% are first generation rich, which means they started with nothing and built up a lot of wealth. Over 300 of the 400 are billionaires. A billion is a thousand million! That's a lot of money. These are not broke people.

I don't know about you, but if I got the chance to sit down and talk with some of these men and women, I would want to ask them how they did it. Lucky for us, because I don't have any of their phone numbers, Forbes asked the questions for us. When asked what **the number one key to building wealth** was, 75% of the Forbes 400 – a supermajority – said it was **becoming and**

staying debt-free. That's the number one key because when you don't have any payments, you suddenly have money. And when you have money, you can do some really smart things, like investing, and become very wealthy.

Why You Should Get Out of Debt Forever

With most Americans not doing a good job of handling their money and almost all of them having an opinion about how you handle yours, you really have to stop and think about where you are getting your financial advice.

If you want to win in any area of your life, you should find people that are winning and do what they're doing. If you weigh 350 pounds and you want to get in better physical shape, don't ask your 350 pound buddy while you're eating a double super-sized value meal together at McDonald's. Instead, head to the gym and find a personal trainer that looks like he could appear on the cover of Men's Health and ask him what you should do.

This is not rocket science and it is especially true in the area of money. So, if you want to win with money, don't ask broke people. This statistically includes most of your parents, grandparents, friends, family, teachers, church members, co-workers, and old college buddies because most of them are broke. Instead, find rich people and ask them what you should do, or keep reading.

Not only can you build a substantial amount of wealth without payments, but imagine the following situation with me for a minute.

What if you had absolutely no payments? No car payments. No credit card payments. No student loans. Imagine having a fully-funded emergency fund in the bank that would cover about six months of living expenses, say $20,000. That would pretty much ensure that you wouldn't have to borrow money when life happens and your car breaks, the heat breaks, or there is a big deductible on your medical insurance. So, with no payments in the world and your income freed up, you are now investing a big chunk of money into your retirement accounts so you would retire with dignity. Since you still had money leftover, you were saving for your kids' college so they don't have the burden of student loans. Imagine having tons of fun and going on vacations that don't follow you home with credit card statements. Now think about keeping your foot on the gas and paying off the house. Absolutely no payments anywhere, not even a house payment! Breathe that in for a moment. That's called freedom. These are the things I want you to accomplish in your life and the process is very simple. The best way to do these things is to stop paying the bank all this interest now.

Freedom comes in the form of you having total control of your life and being able to make choices. If you or your spouse desired to be a full-time mom or dad, you now have the ability to fulfill that dream. You can now be a blessing in the lives of so many people in your family, your community, and the entire world. When you hear about foreclosures on TV, you'll know that you'll never be in that position, because 100% of the foreclosures happen on a house with a

100% of foreclosures happen on a house with a mortgage.

mortgage. After 20 years of instilling these common sense financial principles in your children, when they graduate debt-free, imagine what goals they will be able to accomplish by being financially fit at such an early age. You have just changed your family tree. And it's all because you made the decision not to live like *everyone else* so you could reap the rewards of a lifetime of reduced stress and winning with your money. That's a place worth going!

What it Takes to Get Completely Out of Debt

One indication of successfully making it through the 90 Day Money Challenge is to have a moment of disgust. That's when you take a look at your financial situation and you say, "Enough is enough! I'm not going to live like this anymore! This is stupid! I work too hard and make too much money to be this broke and have nothing to show for it! I'm going to change the things that put me in this condition!"

I'm suggesting that you get angry and frustrated enough with yourself so you're willing to change your life. I don't want you to get so frustrated that you beat yourself up for all of your past mistakes, but if the frustration is enough of an emotion that leads you to change, that's an awesome frustration and it can become the catalyst that causes you to win. Do a harsh financial autobiography and think about how much money you've made in your life and figure out what you have to show for it. After reading this book, you'll find some things that you did that wealthy people don't do. The benefit of having made some mistakes is that you get to learn from them and you can make a list of things you're not going to do anymore. Take that anger at yourself and use it as your motivator to get focused on this process. You're going to win when you have that moment because you will not do the same things anymore.

This journey to get completely out of debt and stay out of

debt forever is going to require passion.

Where does passion come from? Passion is a result. It's the feeling you have when you're engaged in something that you love. It's the reason you can paint your entire body the colors of your favorite team and stand outside wearing almost no clothing in the middle of winter screaming your head off at a ball game. You have passion because you care.

Well, it's time to get passionate and intense about getting out of debt. You'll get out of debt when you take responsibility for your life and your family and decide it's important enough to change your life and not live the way you've been living anymore. When it becomes important enough to you, that's when you'll win.

Think about someone that you care deeply about. Get that person's face in your mind right now. Do you have them pictured? Now pretend that they had some kind of serious medical condition that they could fully recover from if they get a special medicine. And they have to get the medicine within four months or they will die. The medicine costs $5,000 and it's not covered by insurance. You have to get the money, but you don't have it and you can't borrow it. Would you get it? Would you get $5,000 within four months if it meant saving the life of a loved one? The easy answer is yes. You would. Because it was important, you would do it. When getting out of debt is important, you will do it. When you have that moment of disgust and you make the decision to get intense, you're ready to follow the steps to get out of debt.

Step 1: Stop Borrowing

The first step to getting out of debt is to stop borrowing money. You can't get out of a hole while you're digging out the bottom. So, cut up your credit cards. Use your debit card. No more car payments, and pay cash for everything going forward. Everything! I don't care if the company is offering 0% financing. Even at 0%, debt takes control of your income. And the company has to borrow money to lend to you at 0% and they don't pay 0% on borrowed money, so they end up building their costs into the product. When you pay with cash, you can get better deals. For cars and education too! Since we have pledged to borrow no more, saving for things is the only way to make a purchase.

This is not easy. It requires you drawing a line in the sand. You have to have a "no matter what" moment. Never again should you borrow money. No matter what, there is nothing worth borrowing money for that you need. **There is no longer "good debt" and "bad debt."** Avoid all debt at all costs.

Even if you say you pay off your credit card every month (70% of Americans do not pay off their balance *every* month), you should still cut it up and close the account. The average person that uses credit cards spends 12% - 18% more on purchases than a person that uses cash because there is no emotional attachment to a plastic card like there is to cash. Why do you think they use plastic poker chips in Las Vegas? Because people wouldn't spend as much if they used cash. Why do you think McDonalds started accepting credit cards and gave away some of their revenue to credit card companies? Because the average sale went up 47%. Using credit cards is like leaving a loaded gun on the kitchen table. It could go off! I've never met anyone with a bunch of credit card debt that thought it was a good financial plan to go deeply into credit card debt. At the same time, I've never met anybody that didn't use credit cards that had

> *Using credit cards is like leaving a loaded gun on the kitchen table.*

credit card debt. You can do everything with a debit card that you can do with a credit card, except go into debt, so cut the stupid things up!

While we're on the topic of never borrowing money, don't get in the finance business. **Never co-sign.** Most people co-sign for someone at some point in their life and most of the time, they end up paying the bill. Debt is the most marketed product in our culture today. Nothing else is sold with the frequency, sophistication, or financial backing as often and as in your face and as beautifully as debt is. Why do banks sell so much debt? Because it is so profitable. And if these people who are so desperate to sell debt will not loan it to your friend or family member, do you know why? Because they know they are not going to pay the debt. But we think we are so smart that we're going to co-sign. That's stupid. If you co-sign, get ready to pay the bill. Never lend money. If you want to co-sign for someone because you think they're so credit worthy, even though the aggressive debt marketing industry doesn't think so, it's okay to give them some money, but don't lend it. If you don't have the money to give them, then co-signing will be even more of a disaster when the bank comes after you because you're signing up for a debt that you don't have the money to pay. Co-signing means you are also signing.

Step 2: Quickly Save $1,000

The second step to getting out of debt is to quickly save $1,000 for an Emergency Fund. Put this $1,000 in a separate savings account at your bank. The purpose of this $1,000 is to prevent you from having to borrow money the next time life doesn't work out as

Unexpected events do occur. Expect them!

planned. The car's going to break, there will be a medical bill, something will happen, so be prepared. Unexpected events do occur. Expect them!

Don't save more than $1,000 unless you know an emergency is coming, such as a job layoff, transmission slipping, or a baby on the way. When you have more than $1,000 saved, you're not nearly as eager to get out of debt.

Step 3: Debt Snowball

Now that you have committed to staying out of debt and you have your $1,000 saved so you won't have to borrow money next time something goes wrong, it's time to identify the monster.

The third step to getting out of debt is to make a list of all of your debts except your house. List the balance of all of your

www.
Download the Debt Snowball Form!

debts from the smallest balance to the largest. This is called the Debt Snowball and it is the order you will be paying them off. I know it doesn't feel right to

do it this way, but as we have discovered, your feelings can trick you. Mathematically, the best way to pay off your debt is to pay off the highest interest rate first, but if you were doing math, you wouldn't have this debt.

Personal finance is more about behavior than it is about math. Getting out of debt is more like going on a diet and losing weight than it is about finance class in college. You will get out of debt faster when you motivate yourself to pick up the intensity. You need some quick wins in order to stay pumped enough to get out of debt completely. When you start knocking off the easier debts, you will start to see results and you will start to win in debt reduction.

The idea is to stop everything except minimum payments and focus on one thing at a time. Otherwise, nothing gets accomplished because all your effort is diluted. You can wander into debt, but you can't wander out. To get out, you're going to have to be intense and focus on one at a time.

Do not be concerned with interest rates or terms unless two debts have similar payoffs, then list the higher interest rate debt first. Paying the little debts off first gives you quick feedback, and you are more likely to stay with the plan. The positive feedback you give yourself, the sense of traction you begin to feel in your life, the pats on the back you give yourself by knocking off some of your smaller debts supersedes the little bit of interest loss you have by doing it the mathematical way from highest interest rate to lowest interest rate.

I know this is counter-intuitive, but I have been where you are. This process is designed so you do one thing at a time and keep the debt reduction process simple. I know how fast I wanted to get out of debt and I know mathematically, paying off the highest interest rate debt felt right. I know how you feel, and I have learned that what really works is unbelievably fierce, focused intensity.

Step 4: Pick Up the Pace

The fourth step to getting out of debt is picking up the pace. There are three things that you need to do to get out of debt quickly:

1. *Temporarily* pause your investing.
2. Change your withholdings if you are getting big tax refunds.
3. Consider selling everything that's not tied down.

First, it's time to *temporarily* stop all of your investing. What!? Stop investing!? Even if you are getting a match on your company 401(k), you need to stop investing so you can bring home more money to get out of debt quickly.

I understand the power of compound interest and all of the other concepts they taught us in college, but you will end up with more money by getting out of debt very quickly and getting back to investing with way more than you were doing. My best advice for you to become a quality investor is to get out of debt and stay out of debt because your most powerful wealth-building tool is your income. When you don't have any payments, you have the ability to save, invest, give, and spend like no one else.

For example, if you are investing 5% into your company's 401(k) because that is what they match, and if you make $50,000 per year, you are investing $2,500 per year. You are not getting rich off of $2,500 per year, but bringing home an extra $200 per month will really help you get out of debt. If you missed the $2,500 per year for two years while you get completely out of debt, you would have missed $5,000 of investing. But having no payments for the rest of your life will allow you to contribute way more money to investing and you can start investing 15% of your income later on. Without a raise, that's $7,500 per year, which is much easier to do without car payments, credit card payments, and student loan payments, and you will get rich off of $7,500 per year!

Most financial professionals think this is crazy, but **I like the way I get people out of debt more than the way other financial professionals don't.**

Second, stop "investing" in big tax refunds. Most people get a tax refund of $2,000 - $3,000. This is not a gift from Santa Claus. The reason that most people get a tax refund is because they pay too much in taxes. If you are expecting to continue to get tax refunds over $500, you should change your withholdings so you start getting more money in each paycheck and less money at the end of the year. If you normally get a $3,000 tax refund, you could be bringing home another $250 per month and that would really help you get out of debt quicker.

Third, it's time to consider selling everything that is not tied down. There are three different types of things that you should consider selling:

1. Any non-retirement investments.
2. Consider downsizing your vehicles.
3. Miscellaneous items.

First, you should sell any investments that you have that are not in a retirement account. These could be stocks, bonds, mutual funds, saving accounts, etc. This should make immediate sense when you think about it in a different way.

For example, if you had $10,000 in stock and your smallest two debts were a $3,000 credit card and a $12,000 credit card, I suggest that you sell the stock and pay off as much debt as possible. If you sold the stock, you could pay off the $3,000 credit card and pay $7,000 off your $12,000 credit card and only have a $5,000 balance left. I know that's hard to grasp, so let's look at from a different angle. Pretend you only had a $5,000 credit card and you didn't have $10,000 in stock. Would you go borrow $7,000 more on a credit card that you already had a $5,000 balance and $3,000 on a new credit card just to buy $10,000 in stock? The answer is no! You wouldn't. That's the exact reason you should sell any non-retirement investments to pay off debt.

When you think about this scenario from this perspective, you begin to measure risk. Normally, we simply use our head to figure out the math. We think we can invest in stock and get 10% and keep the debt and pay 6%, so we're making out. When you make 10% on stock, you have to pay taxes, so your 10% starts to look closer to 8%. In graduate school finance, students are taught to measure risk, but most people either never take these classes or they forget about them, and when you add risk into the equation, these figures, 6% and 8%, start to look identical. Quit trying to rationalize all of your actions with math!

Quit trying to rationalize all of your actions with math!

If you use this example to think bigger, pretend you had a $200,000 mortgage on a $300,000 house at 5% interest and you had $300,000 in non-retirement investments. If this is you, you should sell $200,000 of the investment and pay off your house today and you will have a paid-for house and $100,000 in the investment. Considering risk allows me to make this decision. If you had $100,000 in investments and a paid-for $300,000 house, would you go borrow $200,000 on your paid-for house just to have $300,000 invested? If you didn't owe anything on your house, would you go borrow on it to invest? No. That's measuring risk. Sell any non-retirement investments and get out of debt right now!

Second, you should consider downsizing in car if you have a car that is worth a lot and you have a lot of debt. For example, if you have a car that is worth $15,000 and you owe $10,000 on it, you could sell it, take the $15,000 and pay off the $10,000 loan, and use the $5,000 left over to buy a $5,000 reliable car with cash. Then you don't have any car payments.

If you owe more on the car than it's worth, you can still sell the car, but you need to come up with the difference. You can do that if you have the cash, save the cash, or you can borrow the difference. I know I said stop borrowing, but you already have car debt and I'm talking about borrowing a little bit to pay off a lot. For example, if you have a car that is worth $15,000 and you owe $17,000 on it, you could borrow $2,000 and sell the car for $15,000. Putting the $2,000 and the $15,000 together, you would be able to pay off your car loan and get the title to the car so you can give it to the buyer. If you are rationalizing not being able to do this because you wouldn't have a car, you could borrow $2,000 more, for a total of $4,000, and buy a $2,000 car. In this case, you would owe $4,000 on a car that is worth $2,000, but $4,000 in debt is a lot better than $17,000 in debt.

Third, you should consider selling anything that you don't want as badly as you want to get out of debt. Look around the house and consider putting everything on Craigslist or eBay that you don't need. Do you have any exercise equipment that you're just using to hang clothes? Do you have an extra TV that you never watch? If you look at something that you could sell for $200 and you would rather be $200 less in debt than have that item, put it up for sale.

Step 5: More Income

The fifth step to getting out of debt is to consider bringing in more money. In the short-term, there are two main ways to do this and both of them don't sound too pleasant.

The first is overtime. If you have the ability, work as much overtime as possible so you never have to work overtime again. If you are sticking to your budget, all of the money you make from working overtime will go straight to whatever goal you are working on at the time. Also, if your company pays you mileage for driving, volunteer to do any errands or events that cause you to drive as much as possible.

The second thing you should consider is working an extra job. This can either be a part-time job or you can turn one of your hobbies into a small business. Usually a small business idea can make a lot more money for your time than punching a clock at Taco Bell, and it can be a lot more fun. Some great examples that you could easily help you earn an extra $500 - $1,000 per month are:

- Cutting grass, lawn care, shoveling snow
- House cleaning
- Pet walking, pet sitting
- Handyman
- Pressure washing and sealing
- eBay merchant
- Professional service (bookkeeper, graphic designer, website developer, any area of expertise can be leveraged into a profitable business)
- Tutoring
- Haul stuff with your truck

Imagine what kind of makeover you could start to give your budget if you took some of these ideas. Let's say you had $100 left over at the end of the month. If you *temporarily* stopped your 401(k) investing and brought home $200 more per month. If you changed your withholdings to stop getting $3,000 tax refunds and brought home $250 more per month. If you started doing a little overtime or started doing some side work and you brought in $500 more per month. All of this would turn your $100 you had left over at the end of the month into $1,050. That's over ten times as much left over. If your first goal was to save $1,000, on your current plan, that would take ten months. By adopting some new ideas, you could have that completed in one month. That's the power of focusing on one thing at a time.

What Not to Do

Midnight cable is full of advertisements that promise to help you get out of debt quickly. You should not work with any of them. The only way you get out of debt is to get intense and take control of the situation yourself.

Debt consolidation companies take all of your debts and roll them into one big loan. It is sold with the benefit of a lower interest rate and a smaller payment. The lower interest rate is usually a bunch of bologna. Most debt consolidation programs give you the average interest rate of all of your debt. It sounds like a deal to get an 8% loan so you can stop paying 18% on a credit card, but you have to throw your 0% loans into the mix. On average, the interest rate you come out with is not better than your average interest rate you are currently paying. Also, smaller payments just lead to more time in debt. If you do a five-year consolidation loan and throw in a debt that was about to be paid off in a few months, you just financed that over five years. Bad idea! The only thing you should ever consider consolidating is all of your federal student loans into one fixed-rate student loan. This truly is an opportunity to get a lower interest rate.

Debt management and debt settlement companies take over payments of all of your debts and collect one monthly payment from you with a huge up-front fee and an ongoing monthly fee. However, they don't pay your debts while they collect the money. They pile it up after they take their big chunk and you end up getting really far behind with all of your creditors. Then the companies try to settle your old, bad debts for pennies on the dollar when the creditors don't think they are going to get paid. This is wrong on so many levels. If you have the money, you have to pay your debts. You don't need to pay a debt management or a debt settlement company to do this for you. The money you would pay them would go a long way to paying off your debts. Don't be wasteful. Also, these companies rarely produce the results that they advertise.

Mortgage accelerator programs carry around the pitch of you being able to pay off your huge mortgage in less than three years. You've definitely seen these ads on TV and they are a waste of money. **The only way to pay down your mortgage faster is by paying extra on the principal. That's it!** The only way to do that is by living on less than you make.

One of the popular mortgage accelerators requires an up-front fee of about $3,000 and they give you their "magic" software where you use a home equity loan to pay your bills and if you live on less than you make, the difference gets applied to your mortgage. You can get the exact same result by living on less than you make and making an extra mortgage payment each month without paying $3,000 for the privilege.

Another popular mortgage accelerator is the bi-weekly mortgage, where you pay a half payment every other week. That would normally pay off a 30-year mortgage in about 23 years. That part is true, but it's not because of any special program. The reason a bi-weekly mortgage payment will pay off your house faster is because you pay 26 bi-weekly payments in a year. 26 bi-weekly payments is equivalent to 13 full payments, which is one more than you would normally pay if you paid once per month. All of the "magic" comes from the extra payment that goes straight to the principal of the loan. You can simply setup your automatic payment to the mortgage company with an extra 1/12th of a normal payment each month and you will get the exact same result, without paying for the program. It's okay if you go with the bi-weekly mortgage payment, but only if it is free when your loan is being setup. Don't pay extra for it!

Speaking of mortgages and options to never consider, here are some additional items:

Never do an adjustable rate mortgage (ARM). An ARM is a home loan secured by a deed of trust or mortgage in which the interest rate will change periodically, usually annually. The banks started using this as a result of high interest rates in the early 1980s as a way for banks to transfer the risk of higher interest rates to the consumer. Basically, you lose control of what can happen if you get an adjustable rate mortgage and the interest may adjust so high that you are no longer capable of making the payment.

Never do an interest only mortgage. This is a bad idea because you are only paying the interest! Most people get one because that's all they can afford at the time, which is a really bad idea. If you can't afford a traditional mortgage payment on the house you want, you're not ready to buy that house.

Never buy rental real estate with debt. Midnight cable advertisements and get rich quick books are full of these "strategies." They will get you caught in a trap.

Never lease a car. Car dealerships push the lease so much because that is what generates the most money. And guess what? If dealerships make the most money, you lose the most money! The main reason that people sign up to lease a car is because it requires a smaller down payment and a smaller monthly payment. **Broke people ask, "how much down, and how much per month?" Wealthy people ask, "how much?"** When you can look past the monthly payment and think longer than one month down the road, you will realize that leasing is the most expensive way to pay for a car.

90 Day Critical Action Steps

☐ Complete your own Debt Snowball by identifying all of your non-mortgage debts and listing them from smallest payoff balance to largest payoff balance.

☐ Stop borrowing money! Cut up your credit cards.

☐ Save $1,000 in a separate account and nickname that account the Emergency Fund. Do not touch this money for anything except an emergency.

☐ *Temporarily* stop all of your investing. This includes retirement, college fund, stocks, bonds, and mutual funds.

☐ Consider changing your withholdings if you are expecting a tax refund of over $500 so you can bring this money into your household throughout the year. Consult your tax preparer before making any changes.

☐ Consider selling anything that you do not want as badly as you want to be out of debt. This includes your vehicles if you do not think you can pay them off within two years.

☐ Consider working extra to speed up your progress by working overtime, a part-time job, or self-employment from home.

6

HOW TO TURN ALL OF YOUR DREAMS INTO REALITY

Building a House

Picture in your mind having to build a brand new $300,000 house from scratch. There is so much to think about. How big will it be? How many stories will there be? How many bathrooms will it have? Will there be a garage? What material are you going to use for the roof? Will you use carpet, hard wood flooring, ceramic tile, or a combination of all of them? That's a lot to think about.

I have never built a $300,000 house, but I do know that before a bulldozer is brought on the lot to start digging the foundation, every single detail is laid out in a blueprint. It doesn't just show how many square feet or how many stories or bathrooms it will have. It doesn't just show the materials for the roof and flooring. It shows everything! Every single piece of plumbing, every electrical outlet, every cabinet, every single detail is measured out because it's a big $300,000 project. It's no coincidence that when the house is completed, it looks exactly like the blueprint.

Why, then, would you not have a plan for the next few years of your finances? If you make $50,000 per year, the next six years of your life is a huge $300,000 project. If you make $100,000 per year, the next three years of your life is a huge $300,000 project. Why would you not have a plan for that?

Steven Covey, in his book The 7 Habits of Highly Effective People, says one of the most important habits of highly effective people is beginning with the end in mind. He is correct when he says that most people gain a sense of who they are from the opinions, perceptions, and paradigms of the people around them. They allow circumstance and conditioning to mold and form who they are and what they achieve. The most effective people, however, shape their own future. Instead of letting other people or circumstances determine their destiny, they mentally plan and then physically create their own positive results. What they have in their mind shapes their future.

In this chapter, you will learn how to take control of your future by building a vision for where you want to be. In all areas of your life, taking charge of this vision will help you achieve your desired results.

Why You Should Build a Long Range Plan

In his book What They Don't Teach You in the Harvard Business School, Mark McCormack shares a study conducted on students in the 1979 Harvard MBA program. The students were asked, "Have you set clear, written goals for your future and made plans to accomplish them?" Only 3% of the graduates had written goals and plans, 13% had goals, but they were not in writing; and 84% had no specific goals at all.

The members of the class were interviewed ten years later, and the results were beyond belief. The 13% of the class who had goals were earning, on average, twice as much as the 84% who had no goals at all. Even more incredibly, the 3% who had clear, written goals were earning, on average, ten times as much as the other 97%! In spite of such proof of success, most people don't have clear, measurable, time-bounded goals that they work toward.

This is one of many examples that prove you will start achieving goals as soon as you have some. It's like Zig Ziglar says, "You go where you aim, and if you aim at nothing, you will hit that too."

You're also going to need a vision of a better future so you can keep your motivation up. When people take their eye off the goal, they end up losing their steam. They forget why they are doing it. A written game plan will remind you why you are sacrificing to win. When you can stay focused on *why* you are doing what you are doing, the "how to stick with it" will automatically start showing up again as new ideas enter your brain from the energy that comes from your dreams and vision of your future.

You will start achieving goals as soon as you have some.

What it Takes to Win With Money

Winning with money is not normal. Most people are broke and if you don't want to be like most people, you are going to have to engage in new activities. Before you can start doing new things, you need to think differently. Wealthy people have a different outlook on life than normal people. They didn't start thinking the way they do when they got wealthy, they got wealthy when they started thinking this way. Here are some of the principles they choose to live their lives by:

To become wealthy, you must be willing to sacrifice to win. You don't have to give up everything fun in your life, but learning to delay pleasure is a sign of maturity. You need to develop the strength to delay pleasure. When most people want something, they're very impulsive and they just go out and get it. That's normal in North America, but it's also normal to be broke. No one wins at anything without sacrifice.

> *No one wins at anything without sacrifice.*

To become wealthy, you must think long-term. In almost every scenario, if it feels good in the short-term and it's bad in the long-term, it's usually a bad idea. And the opposite holds true. If it feels good in the long-term and it feels bad in the short-term, it's usually a good idea. Wealthy people delay pleasure and think long-term so that they can live their dreams. You need to have bigger goals than eating out this week, going on vacation this summer, and an over-blown Christmas this December in order to win.

To become wealthy, you cannot try to keep up with the Joneses. The Joneses are the family that has it all, or so it seems. The BMW in the driveway (leased), the two-story house with the white picket fence (on the verge of foreclosure), the country club membership (two payments behind), and the kids attending private schools (thanks to credit cards). What you don't see is they are just one broken transmission or medical emergency away from hitting total rock bottom. They can't keep up with all the payments of their extravagant lifestyle. **Don't try to keep up with the Joneses; they're broke**!

Finally, to become wealthy, you must expect criticism. Everybody and their mother has an opinion about how you should handle your money, and most of them are broke. Don't take financial advice from broke people. If broke people are making fun of your financial plan, you know you're right on track! It's really hard when all of your friends are out having a party going broke and you are the only one acting responsibly. They will criticize you and make you feel like you are the weird one. Hey, you are, because normal is broke and **being wealthy is weird**. I know I don't want any part of being normal. That's for sure!

If broke people are making fun of your financial plan, you know you're right on track!

You can do this. You can reach your goals. But first you need to decide not to walk around looking like *everyone else* because *everyone else* isn't doing so great.

The following is a list of statements you've heard in the past, possibly ones you've repeated in the past, and for sure ones you will hear again in the future. I suggest you read them out loud. It's like the devil's advocate. It's what broke people say and saying these statements is what causes them to be broke. They're broke because they carry around the mentality that they are not the problem with their money. Once you say them out loud, their power goes away. Later on, when someone says one of them to you, pull out this list. Tell them you've heard that one already.

- Car payments are a way of life.
- You'll always have a car payment.
- You need to build your credit.
- You need a credit card to ___ [insert anything].
- You can use a credit card and just pay it off every month.
- Leasing a car is what sophisticated financial people do.
- If you pay off your house, you'll lose your only tax break.
- You should take out a home equity loan to pay off your debt.

GPS for Money

You know the comfort you feel when you are driving down the road and you know exactly where you are going? I know it's hard to notice. It's easier to think of the discomfort and stress you feel when you don't know where you are going. Being in an unfamiliar area, not knowing where and when you need to turn, not knowing how far away you are from your destination, the street signs are hard to see, and you can't always trust people walking along the street. You find yourself slowing down at every intersection and squinting your eyes as you turn your head to see if this is where you are supposed to turn. This is exactly what navigating your finances feels like without a plan.

A vision for where you are going will look a lot like GPS for driving. When you are driving with GPS, you don't have to guess when and where you will need to turn, and you don't have to guess when you will reach your destination. All of the information is on the screen. You know exactly what step in the directions you are on and exactly how long until you reach the next step.

The beauty of a vision for your financial future is the same as the luxury of GPS when you drive into uncharted territory. Stress is instantly removed when you don't have to worry about each step of the journey simultaneously, just the one step you are currently on. With your finances, you will be much more productive when you don't have to focus on all of the steps at the same time, rather channeling your energies toward one particular goal. Do you ever try to focus on ten things at once? What happens? Nothing gets accomplished. All of the steps in the vision are important, but the power of focus will propel you through them much faster than spreading out all of your effort and energy among multiple goals at the same time.

Laying Out a Proven Step-By-Step Plan

It's time to lay out your vision. Where do you start? What is it that you would like to do with your money? Should you start with saving for a house? Should you work on getting out of debt? How about saving for retirement? Should you start by saving for emergencies? Maybe a college fund? There are many important financial decisions that pull you in different directions.

The best order to tackle all of these financial goals is taught by Dave Ramsey in his amazing book The Total Money Makeover. This is not a process he just made up. Dave has taught this step-by-step, proven process to millions via his radio show, books, Financial Peace University class, live events, and online. Millions of families are doing this step-by-step process and his team has perfected it.

This isn't theory. It's not get rich quick, it's hard, but it's working and families lives' are being changed. Dave calls it the "Baby Steps." He got the name from the movie *What About Bob?* With Bill Murray and Richard Dreyfuss, where the idea is that you can get anywhere you want to go if you just go one step at a time.

There are seven baby steps. Baby Step 1 is called Baby Step 1 because it's first. **And you're not the exception**. Baby Step 4 is called Baby Step 4 because you don't do it until 1, 2, and 3 are done. And you're not the exception. If he wanted Baby Step 4 to be Baby Step 2, he would have called it Baby Step 2. It would have already been moved. They are called the Baby Steps for a specific reason. They're supposed to take you to a place. Just like you don't start doing the framing on a house until the foundation is in, you need to follow these steps in order.

Baby Step 1 - $1,000 to start an Emergency Fund

Baby Step 2 - Pay off all debt using the Debt Snowball

Baby Step 3 - 3 - 6 months of expenses in savings

Baby Step 4 - Invest 15% for Retirement

Baby Step 5 - College funding

Baby Step 6 - Pay off home early

Baby Step 7 - Build wealth and GIVE!

I have studied and practiced this for years and I am fully convinced this is the best way to do it. I have used it in my life and led many people through it. It's not theory, it works! I have a couple of small steps to add in order to help you apply the Baby Steps to your life in an easier way, which includes making sure your checking account has the correct amount, and saving up to pay the down payment on your house.

Before we get started, the first rule is that your long range plan, or vision, needs to be written down, either on the computer or on a pad of paper.

> **www.**
> *Download the Vision Form!*

When you read chapter 4, you created a budget with all of your income at the top of the page and all of your expenses listed down the page. Your total income minus the total of your expenses equaled your disposable income. Disposable income is not "fun" money; "fun" money should be an expense in your budget. Disposable income is the amount of money that you will be able to apply each month to the list of goals you will create.

Goal #1 - Checking Account Buffer

Goal #1 is to make sure you have enough money in your checking account in order to pay your bills on time. If you have overdrawn your checking account, you must stop now. The thing that solves overdrawing your checking account and paying unnecessary fees is what I call the "checking account buffer." Since you are living on a budget where you are not going to be spending more than you are making, you will have enough to pay all of this month's expenses with this month's income, but do you have enough in the checking account to pay all the expenses you need to without waiting on a paycheck? If not, a few hundred dollars more in the checking account will add a lot of peace to your life and you won't have to worry about when you get paid and when a bill is due. If you feel like you have enough now, you are already past this step. If you ever feel stressed about the timing of when a bill is due versus your next paycheck, consider adding more to the checking account. Usually, $500 does the trick.

Goal #2 - $1,000 Starter Emergency Fund

With enough in the checking account, it's time to move onto Goal #2, and that is to save exactly $1,000 and put that into a separate savings account at your bank. This is called the "starter emergency fund." This is the same $1,000 that I discussed in the chapter 5. Since you are not going to borrow money and use credit cards anymore, you will need to be prepared to pay for emergencies that come up with cash. An emergency fund is for those unexpected events in life that you can't always plan for: the loss of a job, a major car repair, an unexpected medical bill, a car insurance deductible, etc. An emergency does not include pizza, sporting tickets, or getting a good deal on anything fun. It's not a matter of if an emergency will occur; it's simply a matter of when it will occur. It's going to rain, so be prepared with your umbrella: your $1,000 emergency fund.

Most financial planners suggest that you have a fully-funded emergency fund of 3 - 6 months of expenses, and I agree with them 100%. You should have that much saved, and you should be doing a lot of other wonderful things, but at this stage, you need to limit the emergency fund to $1,000. I have found that when people set aside more than $1,000, they lose their intensity that gets them through the next few goals. When people have $10,000 set aside, they're not nearly as eager to go do the next step, which is to get out of debt.

If you have enough in your checking account, and you have more than $1,000 saved, lower the amount to $1,000 in your savings account and use that towards whatever long range goal you are working on next. Then, nickname the $1,000 account the "Emergency Fund."

Your bank should offer a high interest savings account or a money market account that pays a decent interest rate, but you're not going to get rich off of the interest on $1,000, so don't worry too much about it.

If you're married, you need to agree with your spouse that neither of you are going to touch this money unless there is an emergency and you both agree it is an emergency before you use the money. If you ever use some or the entire emergency fund, you need to stop working on whatever goal you are currently working on. Go back and fill up the emergency fund to $1,000.

If you don't have this $1,000 yet, you need to get it quickly. This should not take more than one or two months.

As a side note, do not enroll in any bank programs like Bank of America's *Keep the Change* or Wachovia's *Way2Save*. These programs round up each debit card purchase to the nearest dollar amount and transfer the difference from your checking account to your savings account. Banks pitch these programs by saying "saving is a whole lot simpler when you don't have to think about it." What a horrible way to save: not thinking about it! **Wealthy people are very intentional with their savings. You need to be as well**. Save your money on purpose. If you're already enrolled, cancel it.

Goal #3 - Pay Off All Debt Using the Debt Snowball

Now you have enough in the checking account to live off of without worrying about when you are getting paid, and you have your $1,000 set aside in a separate account that you're not going to touch for anything but an emergency. Now it's time to move onto Goal #3, the Debt Snowball, which we covered in chapter 5.

As a review, you're going to list all of your debts, not including a mortgage if you have one, from smallest payoff balance to largest payoff balance and pay them off in that order. The smallest balance should be your number one priority. Don't worry about interest rates unless two debts have similar payoffs. If that's the case, then list the higher interest rate debt first.

Regardless of income, the average person who is working this program pays off all of their debt except their house in 18 - 24 months.

Goal #4 - Fully-Funded Emergency Fund

Now that you are debt-free except the house, it's time for Goal #4 where you go back to that $1,000 emergency fund and raise it up to a real emergency fund of 3 - 6 months of expenses.

To calculate this, use the budget that you created and add up all of your expenses that you consider necessary. Do not count any debt payments, with the possible exception of a mortgage, because they will not be in your budget when you get to Goal #4.

In most households, this is somewhere between $10,000 and $30,000. Imagine having no payments except a house payment and having something like $20,000 in the bank just for emergencies. What could possibly happen in your life that would cause you to have to spend $20,000? Almost nothing! And if you ever have to use any of this money to cover an emergency, since you have no payments, you can quickly fill it back up.

The Goal #4 Fully-Funded Emergency Fund should takeover your $1,000 starter emergency fund and it should be in the same place: either a high interest savings account or a money market account. Don't think of the emergency fund as an investment. **Think of it as insurance so that you never have to borrow money again**. This will free up your income for the rest of your life.

With no payments, this should only take you about four to six months to complete.

Goal #5 - Down Payment Savings

If you do not own a home yet and you are planning on living in the same place for at least five years, now is the time to consider buying a house. Renting for a short period of time is a great idea. People say rent is a waste of money. Usually those people are broke. Consider rent as patience money while you get through these first four goals.

Goal #5 is to save up for your down payment if you do not already own a home. If you already own a home, just skip this step.

Money is made in the real estate business by buying the right property at the right time, not by taking advantage of the market. So, don't rush into buying a house with almost no money down and a payment that is too big while in debt. This mistake can cause you to be broke for a very long time. **You do not need to buy a house when you are in debt** or when you don't have your Goal #4 Fully-Funded Emergency Fund.

Now that you are debt-free except the house and you have your fully-funded emergency fund, your foundation is now laid to start building some serious wealth. With no payments, you should have plenty of money left over. You should have stopped all of your investing while you were getting out of debt and saving your fully-funded emergency fund. Now it's time to get back into investing!

Goal #6 - Invest 15% into Retirement

Goal #6 is to invest 15% of your gross, pre-tax, income into tax favored retirement accounts. If you make $50,000 per year, 15% of that is $7,500, or $625 per month. When you are looking to invest $625 per month, the best place to start is with your company retirement plan, like a 401(k) or a 403(b), if they match your contribution. You should start by going up to the match that they offer. If your company does not match anything, you should move on to the next best retirement option. If your company matches the first 5%, put exactly 5% into the retirement account at work. In our example, 5% of $50,000 per year is $2,500, or about $208 per month.

The reason to start with the company match first is because they match every dollar you put in the account. If they match dollar for dollar, when you invest $2,500 into the account throughout the year, they add $2,500 and your original $2,500 instantly grows to $5,000. That's a 100% return on your investment and that's about as good as it gets.

Since we are shooting for 15% and you already put 5% into the company plan to get the match, the next best place to go is a Roth IRA. A Roth IRA is a special type of retirement plan where you pay taxes now and the money you invest grows tax free! In our example, you still need to invest $5,000 more each year, or about $417 per month. This is the amount you should put into the Roth IRA.

The reason to move to the Roth IRA after you meet the company's match is because when you pick from the investments that your company has, you usually have about 20 - 30 options. When you move to a Roth IRA, you have about 8,000 options and you will find better options. Think of it as picking between a $50 gift card to Outback Steakhouse and a $50 gift card that would work at any restaurant in the world. Which one would you choose? Chances are you would go with the anywhere in the world gift card. Although Outback Steakhouse has 20 - 30 nice things on the menu, if you got to pick from about 8,000 options at all the restaurants in the world, you could probably find something better.

Sorry Outback Steakhouse, I love your food!

When you're ready to invest, I suggest that you get the help of a professional. Even though I know a lot about investing, I still choose to use a professional. Statistics show that "do-it-yourselfers" are quick to jump out of investments when they begin to under-perform. A good professional advisor will remind you why you chose the investment in the first place and prevent you from losing money by buying high and selling low.

A good investment professional will also teach you all about investing. You should follow two simple rules when it comes to investing. First, find a professional that has the heart of a teacher. You will know they have the heart of a teacher when you learn things from them. Sadly, most financial professionals do not. Second, never buy an investment that you don't understand. Before you buy, you must learn about it and other options, and you must be able to explain to a seventh grader how it works. If you can't do that, you're not ready to buy the investment yet.

If you max out your company retirement plan's matching amount (5% in our example) and you are not eligible for a Roth IRA or you max out your Roth IRA contribution and you still have not hit your 15% target, go back to the company retirement plan and continue to increase how much you are putting into that plan until you reach your 15% total target.

To put this into perspective, if you're 30-years-old and you make $50,000 per year now and you get to Goal #6 by getting out of debt, getting your fully-funded emergency fund, and getting into a house within three years, you will be 33. If you began investing 15% of your income, or $7,500 per year, from age 33 to age 67 and you never got a raise, by the time you retired, you would have over $2,000,000! If you have $2,000,000 in your retirement account when you go to retire and you just live off the growth each year, you would be making $200,000 per year! And all this assumes no raise. If you work as hard as you are working for 34 years and you don't get a raise, we have a serious problem.

Goal #7 - College Funding Plans

Now that you are on your way to building some serious wealth for your retirement, Goal #7 is to start saving for your kids college (if you have kids and you want to provide for their college).

The best place to save for college is an Educational Savings Account, ESA, and it works like a Roth IRA does for retirement – you put after tax dollars into it and it grows tax free. The most you can put into an ESA is currently $2,000 per year per child.

Goal #8 - Pay Off the House

With some serious wealth-building taking place now, it's time to move to Goal #8 and attack the mortgage and completely pay off the house. Begin throwing all of your extra money toward the mortgage. You are getting closer to realizing the dream of a life without a house payment.

As an example, if you purchased a $300,000 house and you made a 20% down payment, you would have taken out a

$240,000 mortgage. The principal and interest payment on a 30-year mortgage at 5% interest would be $1,288.37 per month. With no other payments and armed with your fully-funded emergency fund, you are investing 15% of your income into retirement and no more than $2,000 for each of your kids into college funds, you should still have money left over to pay extra on the house. You will also make more money over the coming years, so when you're on a plan, raises turn into quicker and quicker progress. Just think, if you made $12,000 extra dollars a year, that's $1,000 extra dollars per month.

If you never paid extra on that 30-year mortgage, you would pay a total of $463,809, which includes $223,809 of interest and 30 years of bondage. If you average paying an extra $1,500 each month, that 30-year mortgage would pay off in less than nine years, and you would only pay $57,841 in interest, saving you $165,968 in interest and over 21 years in debt.

The next page includes a visual of this explanation in action!

Year	$0 Extra Per Month	$1500 Extra Per Month
1	$236,259	$218,041
2	$232,737	$194,958
3	$228,825	$170,695
4	$224,712	$145,190
5	$220,389	$118,380
6	$215,845	$90,198
7	$211,068	$60,575
8	$206,047	$29,436
9	$200,769	$0
10	$195,221	
11	$189,389	
12	$183,259	
13	$176,815	
14	$170,041	
15	$162,921	
16	$155,437	
17	$147,570	
18	$139,300	
19	$130,607	
20	$121,469	
21	$111,864	
22	$101,768	
23	$91,155	
24	$79,999	
25	$68,272	
26	$55,945	
27	$42,987	
28	$29,367	
29	$15,050	
30	$0	
Total Interest	$223,809	$57,841
*Assuming a 5% fixed interest rate on a 30-year mortgage		

Then with a paid-for house, you would free up the $1,500 per month plus the original $1,288.37 payment for a total of $2,788.37 per month or $33,460.44 per year. That would take you less than three years to save $100,000 if you wanted to move up in house and pay cash for a bigger house.

Can you imagine owning your house within ten years? Well, as the raises really pile on because you have much less stress in your life and you're able to focus on work while you're at work, if you averaged an extra $3,300 per month instead of the $1,500 you were using, that means your house would pay off in under five years!

The average person working this program has their house paid off within seven years. When you have no payments anywhere, especially no house payments, you will really start to enjoy the freedom.

Goal #9 - Maximize Wealth-Building and Giving

When you don't owe anyone a dime, it's time to go back to your retirement accounts and max out all of them.

You have a paid-for house, you're maxing out all of your retirement accounts, you're having lots of fun, you have no payments anywhere, you have a fully-funded emergency fund. Life is looking really good. You need to continue to set goals for big ticket items and other investments that you want to buy, but it's time to get down to doing some serious giving.

You need to be giving the entire time you are working your

way through this process, but now it's time to really step it up.

Giving and serving others is where you'll find your greatest joy and you'll find that when you are able to take your eyes off your situation and win with money. I want you to rock your world not only to completely change your life, but to free you up so you can change the lives of your family and your community.

Your vision should now look like this:

Goal #1 – Checking Account Buffer

Goal #2 – $1,000 Starter Emergency Fund

Goal #3 – Pay Off All Debt Using the Debt Snowball
                    (list each debt from smallest to largest)

Goal #4 – Fully-Funded Emergency Fund

Goal #5 – Down Payment Savings

Goal #6 – Invest 15% into Retirement

Goal #7 – College Funding Plans

Goal #8 – Pay Off the House

Goal #9 – Maximize Wealth-Building and Giving

Next to each goal (and each non-mortgage debt for Goal #3), write down how much the amount you need to complete it. An example might look like this:

Goal #1 – $500	Checking Account Buffer
Goal #2 – $1,000	Starter Emergency Fund
Goal #3 – $800	Capital One Credit Card
$1,200	Best Buy Credit Card
$8,000	Student Loan
$12,000	Car Loan
Goal #4 – $13,000	Fully-Funded Emergency Fund
Goal #5 – N/A	Down Payment Savings
Goal #6 –	Invest 15% into Retirement
Goal #7 –	College Funding Plans
Goal #8 – $240,000	Pay Off the House
Goal #9 –	Build Wealth and Give

Now it's time to add dates. Adding dates to your goals will cause you to build hope. Based on the budget you created in chapter 4, the amount of money you had left over at the end of the month is what you can apply to these goals. Based on how much you have left over, put the number of months it will take you to reach the goal.

For example, let's pretend you are making $50,000 per year and you have $500 left over at the end of the month in your budget, you would be able to reach the Goal #1 $500 Checking Account Buffer in the first month. With that out of the way in the first month, you would be able to save $500 per month for the next two months so you would have your Goal #2 $1,000 Starter Emergency Fund two months after that, in month three.

Then you would be able to send your Capital One Credit Card an extra $500 per month for less than two months, and that would be gone by the fifth month. Then, without the Capital One Credit Card payment, you would have more than $500 per month left over since you no longer have that payment, and more can go to the Best Buy Credit Card. If the Capital One Credit Card minimum payment was $50, you now have $550 extra you can send to the Best Buy Credit Card on top of your regular payment. That would cause the Best Buy Credit Card to be paid in less than two more months, almost at the end of the seventh month, and you wouldn't have that payment anymore, probably another $50.

Then you have $600 left over each month and you can start to attack your student loan. If your student loan payment was $200 per month, now you are paying $800 per month. It will take about nine months to pay off an $8,000 student loan, because you paid your normal payment for seven months, which knocked down the balance by about $1,000. By month 16, the student loan is gone. Then you can keep going and add $800 per month on top of your car payment, which is probably $400 per month.

Being 16 months into your plan and paying your car payment on time, the balance on that loan is probably not $12,000 anymore, it's more like $6,600. Now you can start paying $1,200 per month instead of $400 per month and pay off the car in about five months, or by month 21. In less than two years, you could be completely debt-free except your house.

If you determine that you need $13,000 for your Goal #4 Fully-Funded Emergency Fund and you already have $1,000, you need $12,000 more. Ten months of saving $1,200 per month would get you there. Here you are, 31 months into your plan, just 2.5 years, and you just paid off $22,000 in debt, saved a $13,000 emergency fund, and freed up $1,200 per month. Great job! You're now able to easily find 15% of your income, or $625 per month out of the $1,200 that is left over, and begin investing in retirement. **You will be well on your way to becoming a multi-millionaire.**

You Choose How Fast You Go

Do you like the fact that it took 31 months to accomplish all of that? If you're okay with it, I'm okay with it. But if you were able to buckle down and tighten up the budget and free up $1,000 per month instead of $500 per month, it would have taken you a lot less time.

You would have had your Goal #1 $500 Checking Account Buffer in two weeks. It would have taken one month after that to complete your Goal #2 $1,000 Starter Emergency Fund. Your small credit card would be paid off in month three and your larger credit card would have been paid off in month four. The student loan would be gone by month nine and the car would be paid off by month 14, completing Your Goal #3 Debt Snowball. Finally, by month 21, you would have your Goal #4 Fully-Funded Emergency Fund completed. You could have the same result in well under two years.

31 months or 21 months: you get to choose how fast you go. What's that? You don't like 21 months? You can choose to go faster. This section is designed to give you all kinds of suggestions to get the amount of disposable income left at the bottom of the page bigger because the bigger you get that number, the faster you get through the foundational Goals #1 - 4.

As a review from chapter 5, you should do four things to

pick up your pace.

1. *Temporarily* stop all of your investing until you reach Goal #6 Invest 15% into Retirement. Even if you are getting a match from your company, stop investing!
2. Change your withholdings on your W-4 form at work if you are expecting to continue to get big tax refunds over $500. Consult your tax preparer before making any changes.
3. Sell everything that you don't want as badly as you want to get out of debt, including investments and big ticket items such as extra cars, boats, and furniture.
4. Work overtime, get a part-time job, or turn a hobby into a small business for some extra income. Consider using your vacation time at work to be able to work that extra job with more hours.

After you consider these four things, go through every item in your budget with a fine-toothed comb and see what you can lower. Here are some ideas:

☐ Find $20 worth of coupons per month for groceries and toiletries you already buy.

☐ Pack a lunch so you don't eat out during the week.

☐ Split a meal when you eat out.

☐ Lower your electric bill by locking in a lower rate with a different electric provider.

☐ Make sure you are getting your company discount on your cell phone if your cell phone provider has one – the average discount is 15% - 21%.

- ☐ Remove any features you don't need from your cell phone like data packages or unlimited features.
- ☐ Determine if it makes sense to move to a cell phone plan with fewer minutes.
- ☐ Remove premium cable channels.
- ☐ Ask your cable company for a preferred customer discount or consider switching to their competitor; the normal discount is at least $20 per month.
- ☐ Determine if it makes sense to bundle your cable and internet together in the same package.
- ☐ Cancel your house phone; it may be cheaper to add minutes to your cell phone plan.
- ☐ Get three new quotes on term life insurance.
- ☐ Get three new quotes on your auto insurance.
- ☐ Get three new quotes on your homeowner's insurance.
- ☐ Use the flexible spending account at work if they offer it for healthcare costs.
- ☐ Cancel monthly and annual subscriptions.
- ☐ Lower your gifts and Christmas budget while you are getting out of debt.
- ☐ Cancel your gym membership and work out at home.
- ☐ Find ways to save on entertainment, like using Redbox instead of going to the movies.
- ☐ Cancel your house cleaning service.
- ☐ Cut your own grass.
- ☐ Clean out your storage unit and get rid of it.
- ☐ Don't go on vacation this year.

- ☐ Determine if it makes sense to refinance your mortgage only if you are going to get a lower interest rate and do not take any cash out of your house.
- ☐ Sell or donate your timeshare.
- ☐ Cut your own hair.
- ☐ Park farther from work and walk to avoid paying for parking.

Snapshot of the Author's Budget Before and After Changes		
	BEFORE	AFTER
Normal Take Home Pay	$4,800	$4,800
Temporarily Pause Retirement *	$0	$500
Change Withholdings **	$0	$250
Extra Work ^	$0	$600
Total Income	$4800	$6,150
"Necessary" Household Expenses ^^	$2,200	$1,950
Work Lunches	$180	$0
Work Parking	$160	$0
"Irregular" Savings	$100	$0
Car Minimum Payment #	$378	$0
Other Debt Minimum Payments	$448	$448
Miscellaneous "Fun" Money +	$1,334	$200
Total Expenses	$4,800	$2,598
Extra to Pay Off Debt	$0	$3,552

* *Temporarily* stopped investing into retirement

** Changed withholdings on W-4 form

^ Worked extra and got paid for voluntary travel (mileage)

^^ Implemented many of the budget savings ideas from previous page

\# Sold 4-Runner and used cash from savings to buy a $3,000 Honda

\+ We didn't know where our money was going before we did a budget but we were spending it somewhere (we skipped a summer vacation)

Note: this does not include a $2,000 tax refund or a $2,000 work bonus we received while getting out of debt.

When to Pause Progress on Your Vision

If you are working on your Goal #3 Debt Snowball, you should stop paying extra on your debt and instead start piling up money in your emergency fund if you are in the middle of an emergency or there is a potential emergency on the horizon. These include, but are not limited to job layoff, a major car repair, a major medical bill coming in, a pregnancy, and a car accident where you will have to pay a deductible.

Once the emergency passes and you are able to continue living on less than you make and you're not incurring any new debt, like a medical bill, lower your emergency fund back to the Goal #2 $1,000 level and take any money you piled on top of that and start paying off your debts in your Goal #3 Debt Snowball from smallest balance to largest.

Celebrating Your Victories

As you hit each big goal, and each sub-goal inside of the Goal #3 Debt Snowball, celebrate! You deserve it. Keep the celebrations fairly small until you are past Goal #4 Fully-Funded Emergency Fund, but then make the celebrations pretty big. When you get past Goal #4 Fully-Funded Emergency Fund and you are out of debt except for your house with somewhere between $10,000 and $30,000 in savings, that puts you in the top 10% of Americans. Now you are embarking on a path to move to the top 2.5% of Americans, which are millionaires!

When you complete Goal #8 Pay Off the House, you need to have a big mortgage-burning party. That's where you invite your friends and family over and you burn the mortgage paperwork in the back yard. As part of the festivities, you need to take your shoes and socks off and walk across the backyard, because the grass feels different when it's yours!

90 Day Critical Action Steps

- ☐ Create your written long range plan. Don't change the order from the following unless you have a really good reason, but insert goals where necessary:
    - ☐ Goal #1 – Checking Account Buffer
    - ☐ Goal #2 – $1,000 Starter Emergency Fund
    - ☐ Goal #3 – Pay Off All Debt Using the Debt Snowball (list each debt)
    - ☐ Goal #4 – Fully-Funded Emergency Fund
    - ☐ Goal #5 – Down Payment Savings
    - ☐ Goal #6 – Invest 15% into Retirement
    - ☐ Goal #7 – College Funding Plans
    - ☐ Goal #8 – Pay Off the House
    - ☐ Goal #9 – Maximize Wealth-Building and Giving
- ☐ Go through all of the ideas in the checklist in the "You Choose How Fast You Go" section of this chapter to speed up your progress.
- ☐ Based on how much money is left over in your budget (disposable income), put an expected completion date next to each goal.

7

HOW TO ENSURE SUCCESS WITH THIS CHALLENGE

Weight Watchers

Weight Watchers has a fabulous weight loss program. Research shows that people who attend Weight Watchers meetings lose three times more weight than those who diet on their own. That is a great track record. But Weight Watchers doesn't sell magic food. In fact, no food is off limits! And Weight Watchers doesn't force you to work out with personal trainers. So, why is it that individuals who use the Weight Watchers plan see such remarkable results?

Weight Watchers' core approach is to assist members in losing weight by eating smarter, getting more exercise, forming helpful habits, and providing support. Everyone knows that eating smarter and getting more exercise will cause you to lose weight, but that doesn't cause people to do it. The difference is the combination of forming helpful habits and providing support. Living on a budget, getting out of debt, and building a vision are the helpful habits that cause you to win with your money, but the glue that holds all of them together is getting support.

The main reason people lose weight on the Weight Watchers program is not because they get a breakthrough in knowledge that eating a bunch of fatty foods and never exercising causes you to become fat, it's because when you know you have to go to your Weight Watchers meeting and get on the scale on Monday night, it's a lot easier to pass up on dessert on Sunday night. Knowing that your progress toward your goals will be measured is one of the most positive forms of behavior modification ever invented.

Building New Habits is a Process

Most people see life as a bunch of events, not a process. Everything in life is an event or a destination. We have vacations, birthday parties, and anniversaries. These are events and they are what we look forward to. Reading this book is an event. Unfortunately, reading this book will do you no good whatsoever unless you're going to change the way you're living your financial life. Reading this book doesn't change anything. The process is what changes things.

Getting in good shape is not an event. It's a process. Weight loss is not an event, it's a process. Living on a plan is not an event, it's a process. Getting out of debt is not an event, it's a process. Learning to handle your money well is not an event, it's a process. So, you need to engage in this process to be able to win.

Learning to handle your money well is not an event, it's a process.

The best way to build these habits into your life and stick

with your plan to live on a budget, get out of debt, and set and achieve goals is to hold yourself accountable. Once you have created an action plan, ultimately you are responsible for carrying out the plan, but effective people choose to enlist the help of others. Knowing that your progress is going to be measured will cause you to make progress. Accountability will change your life! So, you have to put yourself in that kind of position to change your finances.

Why You Should Implement Accountability

An accountability partner or a support team can do many wonderful things to help you reach your goals. These individuals can provide valuable resources and offer encouragement and can help you succeed in your efforts.

Working with a support system can help you by listening to your struggles and being a cheerleader for your victories. They can pose questions that will help you clarify your goals. They can challenge you and help advise you in difficult times. They can shed light on your situation and provide a different perspective. They can offer you a reality check when you are trying to rationalize a bad habit. They can instill confidence and motivate you to keep going. **Encouragement and accountability will help you stick with your plan when life gets tough**. Finally, they can periodically follow-up with you to make sure you are sticking to your plan.

Accountability partners are not just for single people. Accountability partners or accountability couples can help married people just as much. If you are married, you need to find an accountability partner or an accountability couple that is agreeable to both of you. There are no excuses for avoiding implementing accountability into your financial plan.

Qualities of Your Accountability Partner

Since most people in America are **physically** overweight and out of shape, most people don't qualify to be your physical trainer. In the very same way, since most people in America are **financially** overweight and out of shape, most people do not qualify to be your financial accountability partner. Your accountability partner needs to be four things:

1. Personally responsible.
2. Positive.
3. Someone you respect.
4. Someone local that you can meet with one-on-one.

First, your accountability partner needs to exemplify personal responsibility. John Miller wrote the book QBQ, which is all about purging the three enemies of personal responsibility: blame shifting, complaining, and procrastination. People that think their problems lie outside of themselves, and are always pointing the finger at someone else, will not understand your motivation to fix your own problems. People that complain all the time usually don't want their problems solved because then they wouldn't have any reason to complain. They will not understand your desire to get in the driver's seat of your life. People that tend to procrastinate will not be good accountability partners because if they don't have the motivation to get in the driver's seat of their lives and get things done, they will not be a good fit to take charge and hold you accountable when you are facing difficult times.

Second, your accountability partner needs to be a positive person. You must keep away from negative people, even negative family members. Instead, you need to get positive influences in your life and tell them what you're doing. When you tell someone that has a good view on life how you are taking control of your life, they will join your team.

As children, we heard, "Sticks and stones may break my bones, but words will never hurt me." That is just flat out wrong. No matter who you are, negative words can really drag you down. Someone speaking something positive into your life is a lot different than someone speaking something negative in your life. A little positive comment can motivate you beyond belief.

Also, you become who you hang around with. You knew that. But look around you. Are you surrounded by people who are winning? Author of 48 Days to the Work You Love, Dan Miller, says that your personal income will be within 10% - 20% of your ten closest friends' average income. Think of your closest ten friends right now, guess what their income is, and you're going to be within 10% - 20% of that. **You become who you hang around with**. If you hang out with drug addicts, you will become a drug addict. If you run around with people who are winners, you will become a winner. If you run around with people who are gossips, you will become a gossip. If you run around with people who are in shape, you will have a tendency to work out, get in shape, and stay in shape. It's the weirdest thing. If you want to be a positive person, you need to surround yourself with positive people.

Third, your accountability partner needs to be someone

that you deeply respect. Someone that you respect will cause you to reach your goals faster than you would on your own. You won't want to let them down by not following through with the plan that you chose to implement. Your accountability partner must love you enough to be brutally honest and promise to do so for your own good.

Fourth, your accountability partner needs to be someone that is local, that you can meet with one-on-one. You should plan to meet with your accountability partner on occasion and that can be very difficult if they don't live near you. This needs to be someone you can discuss your budget and long range vision with. You can keep the level of detail to whatever you want (such as specific numbers on income or debts), but they need to know what your goals are, when you expect to hit them, and how you are doing compared to your plan. Having a local accountability partner is also going to come in handy when you begin reaching your goals. After you reach each goal or pay off each debt, you will need someone that you can share your success with. Sharing your victory stories will really help keep you motivated to continue on your path to financial fitness.

Your Accountability Relationship

When you find your accountability partner and they agree to help hold you accountable to reach your goals, walk through the following three-step process before you get started:

1. Explain what you are doing and why you are doing it.
2. Share your goals and your plan to reach them.
3. Establish a time and place to meet.

First, tell them what you're doing with your money and what you are looking for in an accountability relationship. Explain to them how you are looking to modify your behaviors because you want to win with your money and that their support is very important to you reaching your goals. Tell them that you now have a new way of looking at your finances. Tell them how you don't want to be normal, because normal stinks. Most importantly, **tell them *why* you are doing what you are doing**. Tell them how you are going to get on a written plan to get out of debt so you can free up your largest wealth-building tool, your income. Tell them that following through with your plan will enable you to live with less stress, retire early with mega-dignity, travel anywhere you want, change your family tree, and leave a legacy.

Second, walk them through your step-by-step plan with the specific goals in your vision. Get them to understand that the only way you are going to reach your goals is to stick to your written monthly budget. Ask them to hold you accountable for three things: that you complete a written budget every single month, that you hit your monthly goal for how much progress you make toward your long range vision each month, and that you are acting on your checklist of recommendations.

Third, establish a specific time and meeting place to meet in person for the first 90 days to follow-up and evaluate your progress. After the first 90 days, establish a time (preferably once each month) to meet in person or on the phone.

If you are having trouble finding an accountability partner, consider your pastor, parents, relatives, supervisor, and your most successful friends if they meet the criteria in the Qualities of Your

Accountability Partner section.

90 Day Critical Action Steps

☐ Identify one person/couple who can help hold you accountable.

☐ Ask that person to hold you accountable during your 90 Day Money Challenge.

☐ Share your long range vision with your accountability partner.

☐ Establish a time and a place to meet with your accountability partner at least once each month.

☐ At each meeting with your accountability partner, discuss your progress from last month and your goals for next month.

8
TRANSFORMED

Don't Be "Normal"

When you believe what *everyone else* believes and you do what *everyone else* does, you are conforming to society's standards and you are going to get what *everyone else* gets: you will be normal. Being normal or mediocre in any area of your life, especially with your money, stinks.

After reading this book, you now know how money should be handled based on what people, who have money, do. By organizing this information in a step-by-step, proven process, I challenge you to get started. Whether this works or not is no longer in question. The only question is, are you going to do it? You can do this stuff! You can rock your world, your kids' world, your grandkids' world, and the world of people throughout your community if you'll act on this! But it's now up to you.

If you build the habits from this book into your life, you

will beat debt and build wealth. It will not happen instantly, but it will happen. When you do, you need to understand that wealth is not an escape mechanism; it is instead a tremendous responsibility. If you think your life is going to get better just because you have money, you're wrong.

There are only three things you can do with money: you can have fun with it, you can invest it, and you *Giving is the* can give it. And you need to be doing all three. *most fun* Giving is the most fun you'll ever have with *you'll ever* money. You need to be giving the entire time *have with* you are building wealth, but when good people *money.* get good money, they can change the world.

Be "Weird"

If normal stinks, setting out to be weird is a great goal to shoot for. Be willing to be weird! The way you become weird and change the way you act is to transform the way you think: change the way you look at the world by putting new information into your mind.

The average millionaire reads at least one non-fiction book per month. If you want to be wealthy, you need to do what wealthy people do. Charlie "Tremendous" Jones says, "Five years from today, you will be the same person you are today, making the same money you are today, with the same problems you have today, except for the books you read and the people you meet." You need to be reading some different books and meeting some new people. When you finish school, you have just started a life of learning, because knowledge is the currency of the new economy.

Don't wake up five years from now and wish you changed your life. *Start right now!*

One Last Thing

May I ask you a favor?

If you got anything out of this book (if you highlighted, underlined or took notes), I'm hoping you will do something for me. Give this copy to someone else. Challenge them to read it and ask themselves if there is something they could be doing better.

We need them to have a bigger plan for their future so they change the way they think about money. When they do that, they will change the way they handle money and live much better lives. Marriages will be saved and stress will be significantly reduced. They will change their family trees forever and impact their communities. Just think, if they handle money the right way long enough, they can join you in leaving a legacy and having a positive impact on the world!

Please spread the word. *Thanks!*

9

FREE RESOURCES TO KEEP YOU ON TRACK

For more

Crystal Clear Direction,
Motivation to Act, and
An Environment That Holds You Accountable

Sign up for free at:

www.90DayMoneyChallenge.com

90 DAY
MONEY
CHALLENGE
COMMITMENT

I commit to spending the next 90 days of my life to taking control of my financial future.

_____

Your Name

_____

Spouse's Name (if married)

_____

Accountability Partner/Couple

90 DAY MONEY CHALLENGE

WEEKLY GUIDE

Week 1

☐ Find out how well you are doing by creating a Net Worth Statement. Make a list of all of your assets (houses, cars, savings accounts, checking accounts, retirement accounts, non-retirement investments, etc.) and a list of all of your debts (mortgages, car loans, credit cards, bank loans, personal loans, student loans, etc.). Then, subtract your total debt from your total assets. This is your net worth.

☐ Create a written budget for this month, not the average month. This can be on paper or on the computer. If you don't know how much you are going to spend in a category, make your best guess.

☐ If you're married, you need to agree on the budget with your spouse before you begin spending any more money.

☐ Complete your own Debt Snowball by identifying all of your non-mortgage debts and listing them from smallest payoff balance to largest payoff balance.

☐ Stop borrowing money! Cut up your credit cards.

Week 2

☐ Create your written long range plan. Don't change the order from the following unless you have a really good reason, but insert goals where necessary:

    ☐ Goal #1 – Checking Account Buffer

    ☐ Goal #2 – $1,000 Starter Emergency Fund

    ☐ Goal #3 – Pay Off All Debt Using the Debt Snowball
                 (list each debt)

    ☐ Goal #4 – Fully-Funded Emergency Fund

    ☐ Goal #5 – Down Payment Savings

    ☐ Goal #6 – Invest 15% into Retirement

    ☐ Goal #7 – College Funding Plans

    ☐ Goal #8 – Pay Off the House

    ☐ Goal #9 – Maximize Wealth-Building and Giving

☐ Based on how much money is left over in your budget (disposable income), put an expected completion date next to each goal.

☐ Keep track of all of your expenses for each category.

☐ Pick at least one category to try the cash envelope system.

☐ Stick to your budget. This gets easier and easier over the first 90 days.

Week 3

☐ Save $1,000 in a separate account and nickname that account the Emergency Fund. Do not touch this money for anything except an emergency.

☐ *Temporarily* stop all of your investing. This includes retirement, college fund, stocks, bonds, and mutual funds.

☐ Consider changing your withholdings if you are expecting a tax refund of over $500 so you can bring this money into your household throughout the year. Consult your tax preparer before making any changes.

Week 4

☐ Identify one person/couple who can help hold you accountable.

☐ Consider selling anything that you do not want as badly as you want to be out of debt. This includes your vehicles if you do not think you can pay them off within two years.

Week 5

☐ Ask the person who you would like to be your accountability partner to hold you accountable during your 90 Day Money Challenge.

☐ Establish a time and a place to meet with your accountability partner at least once each month.

☐ Consider working extra to speed up your progress by working overtime, a part-time job, or self-employment from home.

☐ After the 1st month is over, create a budget for the 2nd month. By keeping track of what you actually spend in the 1st month, creating the budget for the 2nd month should be a lot easier.

Week 6

- ☐ Share your long range vision with your accountability partner.
- ☐ Stick to your budget.
- ☐ Cancel your house cleaning service.
- ☐ Get three new quotes on term life insurance.
- ☐ Get three new quotes on your auto insurance.
- ☐ Get three new quotes on your homeowner's insurance.

Week 7

- ☐ Make sure you are getting your company discount on your cell phone if your cell phone provider has one – the average discount is 15% - 21%.
- ☐ Remove any features you don't need from your cell phone like data packages or unlimited features.
- ☐ Determine if it makes sense to move to a cell phone plan with fewer minutes.
- ☐ Remove premium cable channels.
- ☐ Ask your cable company for a preferred customer discount or consider switching to their competitor; the normal discount is at least $20 per month.
- ☐ Determine if it makes sense to bundle your cable and internet together in the same package.
- ☐ Cancel your house phone; it may be cheaper to add minutes to your cell phone plan.

Week 8

- ☐ Lower your electric bill by locking in a lower rate with a different electric provider.
- ☐ Pack a lunch so you don't eat out during the week.

- ❑ Split a meal when you eat out.

Week 9

- ❑ Find $20 worth of coupons per month for groceries and toiletries you already buy.
- ❑ Cancel monthly and annual subscriptions.
- ❑ After the 2nd month is over, create a budget for the 3rd month. By keeping track of what you actually spend in the 2nd month, creating the budget for the 3rd month should be a lot easier.

Week 10

- ❑ At each meeting with your accountability partner, discuss your progress from last month and your goals for next month.
- ❑ Stick to your budget.
- ❑ Cancel your gym membership and work out at home.

Week 11

- ❑ Park farther from work and walk to avoid paying for parking.
- ❑ Use the flexible spending account at work if they offer it for healthcare costs.

Week 12

- ❑ Determine if it makes sense to refinance your mortgage only if you are going to get a lower interest rate and do not take any cash out of your house.
- ❑ Lower your gifts and Christmas budget while you are getting out of debt.
- ❑ Find ways to save on entertainment, like using Redbox instead of going to the movies.

Week 13

☐ Create a budget every single month for the rest of your life. This will become a habit after a few months and once it is a habit, it will be very easy to do.

☐ Find out how well you did during your 90 Day Money Challenge by updating your Net Worth Statement.

☐ Give this book to someone else. Challenge them to read it and ask themselves if there is something they could be doing better.

☐ Keep going! The hard part is now behind you.